THE

UNEXPECTED

MOTHER

THE

UNEXPECTED

MOTHER

A MEMOIR

A Surrogate Mother Caught Between
Science, the Law, and Humanity

SUSAN A RING

Full
Circle
Press

Full Circle Press books may be purchased for other educational, business, or sales promotional use. For further information, please e-mail us at fullcirclepress01@gmail.com Los Angeles, California

SECOND EDITION

Book Jacket, Pictures and Page Design:
Susan A Ring - Los Angeles, California

Library of Congress Cataloging-in-Publication
Data is available upon request.

ISBN 978-0-692-78546-1

For my husband, Paul

My children, Brian, Steven, Nevaeh

and my surrogate children, Evan,

Megan, Matthew and Little One

~ With love and gratitude

Contents

AUTHOR'S NOTE

This book details my journeys as a surrogate mother along with the impossible challenges and circumstances that happened, as a result of my choices, to help intended parents grow their families. I share my story with unflinching honesty. It contains heartbreaking, mature and sexual scenes.

While my story has been told many times on television, including PBS's *Bloodlines*, Dr. Oz, and Dr. Phil with various other news stations and in magazines, including O, The Oprah Magazine (Dec, 2003), O's Top Ten Anniversary Special (May, 2010), and People Magazine, (March 2016), along with international magazines, none told the entire story.

It's important to note that I was a surrogate mother and gave birth to eight surrogate babies, two singletons and three sets of twins for five different families throughout an entire decade of my life, all of my forties. Each surrogacy endeavor is called a *journey*. Each of my five journeys as a surrogate mother were different and unique. Book One, *The Unexpected Mother,* is about my first two surrogate journeys. Book Two, *When Hope Becomes Life,* is about my experience with O Magazine's photo shoot and the next three surrogate journeys, and Book Three, *Full Circle,* details my life after surrogacy, when I was still not able to give up pregnancy even after finding the love I craved. The consequences are life-threatening and bring me full circle, leaving me infertile.

In writing this book I relied on my notes, personal journals, many paper napkins, consultations with people who appear in the book, and calling up my own memories of these events. I have changed the names of most individuals in this book and, in some cases, modified identifying details to preserve anonymity. There are no composite characters or events in this book.

"If we are brave enough often enough, we will fall; this is the physics of vulnerability." ~ Brene Brown

PART ONE

1

Final Word

After what could have been considered a good first journey as a surrogate mother with Michael and Jackie, the second one came crashing down the evening of September 10, 2001, when I heard Jackie's gruff, emotionless voice on the telephone saying, "I don't want the twins. That's it. I'm done. I'm divorcing Michael and moving to Boston with Evan."

My heart skipped a beat as I caught my breath trying to find a way to respond. I didn't know what to say. All I could think of was the way Jackie said to me many times before we started the surrogacy process, "All we've ever wanted was a family, a big family." I laid my hand on my large, growing belly and felt the twins moving inside of me.

I could hear Evan crying in the background of their luxury apartment with multiple large gardens of beautiful, colorful flowers and overflowing foliage on the west side of Los Angeles. Evan was my first surrogate experience, their first baby. I'd given birth to him for Michael and Jackie just short of a year before. Next month would mark his first birthday. Our first journey with Evan went fairly well, which is why we chose to work together again.

I knew she wasn't going to listen to anything I had to say.

Michael was on the other line and remained quiet. Not. One. Single. Word. I honestly didn't hear much past, "...don't want the twins."

"What?" I said in a faint whisper of disbelief.

"Oh, and just be forewarned, Susan, Michael has some psychological challenges he's working on. I used to be able to control it on a daily basis with my nursing experience, but now I cannot and will not. It's between you two."

"I do not, I'm fine, never been better," Michael chimed in. "I have a lot of new ideas for my work."

"Wait, what?" I mumbled and blinked hard a few times and thought, *they don't want the twins? How could this happen?* I noticed my mouth was wide open at the shock of it all. I consciously closed it. Everything I thought beautiful about surrogacy was unraveling. The days of yearning to help another couple have a child felt heavy and daunting. Something felt lodged in my throat. My mind felt like it went blank and I didn't know what to think. Thoughts of self-doubt, not being enough, filled my foggy brain. I wasn't that close to Michael and Jackie but I had no idea he might have psychological problems.

I thought back throughout the time I was a surrogate for them with Evan, and recalled maybe one or two times that Michael had a strange faraway sort of look during a conversation. Sometimes he wouldn't answer a question when directly asked, like he was thinking about what was said, and then didn't answer. It didn't seem like any problem of sorts. I thought maybe it was because he was on medication at the time. My mind was getting ahead of me. I didn't even know if he was medicated or what he had but fear of the unknown started to take over. I wondered if he was seeing a doctor or if his psychological issues were diagnosed? My biggest fear is people who do weird, strange things or have mental disorders. You never know what they are going to do especially if they are off meds. I guess this could be the same for normal people, but the risks go up for people who have mental disorders. This type of thing should have been revealed a long time ago during the matching process. I should have been told that Michael had a psychological disorder. They did a psychological check on me, but I found out later the agency did not do one on Michael or Jackie.

I was not on a best friend basis with Michael and Jackie, but I thought we might be better friends after I carried their child. Were we friends at all? I wondered. Not now for sure. But something—something I couldn't put my finger on—was never quite right throughout our first journey, and I didn't listen to my instincts telling me more than once to move on if I wanted to be a surrogate again, and be one for someone else. I didn't listen to my own intuition.

Michael interrupted my thoughts and said, "I'm working on a new gig for some big executives in Hollywood and money should be better. Please don't go, Jackie, I'll make more money I promise," he pleaded.

We had a contract for God's sake. It felt like they were trying to get out of it. Out of the responsibility of parenting the children they created that were in my body. This didn't seem real. Was I that naïve? How could this happen?

I imagined the whole argument going on for who knows how long. Evan was still crying. My motherly instinct felt a need to hold him. I was helpless to protect him or care for him, but he wasn't my responsibility. My hand went to my belly wondering about how the twins would be cared for. For some strange reason when Jackie denied the twins and said she didn't want them, it felt like they'd automatically become mine. But I pushed that thought away because I became a surrogate mother to help another couple have a child, not become a mother again. I wanted to help others experience the love and joy of having a family. My hands were full being recently divorced and a single mother with two children of my own.

"Right, Michael, call me in Boston when you make

something, anything worthwhile," Jackie snapped. Her voice was stern, uncaring.

"You can't do this, Jackie. Seriously," I managed to say.

"Oh, but I am doing it and some is already done," she said.

Evan, the twins, and I were in the middle of their argument. I was learning that when an embryo belonging to someone else was transferred into my body, I was automatically propelled into the personal life of the intended parents, and their reality became my own, along with their choices and decisions, even if I didn't agree with them. I'd become an intricate and intimate part of their lives by becoming their surrogate mother.

It was my body, but it was their baby.

The next morning was September 11, 2001. I was still in a state of shock, and deep disbelief. It all felt like a nightmare. I repeated over and over again, "How could they?"

I woke up early that morning and stared out the window of my bedroom thinking for hours. I was tired and yet I couldn't sleep. Thoughts I had from our conversation were dangling with no hope of answers any time soon. I was worried about what might happen to the twins, to me, and to Evan. *How could they do this?* I kept repeating in my head. Anxiety filled my thoughts. There would be lifelong decisions we would need to make. *What are we—no, scratch that—what am I going to do?* I realized that although the three of us had entered a contract, I was the only one left in it. Michael and Jackie had already abandoned their children before they were even born. They were full biological siblings to Evan, with the same donor's egg and Michael's sperm.

I looked down and patted my swollen pregnant belly with one hand on the top and one on the bottom and whispered one thing I knew for sure, "Don't worry, I'll take care of you. No matter what." The sun was coming up pushing its way forth as it does every single morning. Pregnancy was like that,

I thought. It was as natural as nature and pushes its way into the world. I lay back down with my hands on my tummy still thinking, wondering if I could have done something different. I was feeling stressed and needed to relax. My monkey mind was moving so fast with too many thoughts but yet I wanted to sleep. I was so tired.

A short month ago, the agency we were working with informed me that Michael and Jackie didn't want the twins and were having financial issues, but the parents never told me directly. I just didn't want to believe it. I thought maybe they were just having a hard time being new parents to Evan. Maybe they were stressed and would change their minds again soon. A glimmer of hope resurfaced in my mind, and fell as fast as the idea of hope came. Because that's what I did, it was my go-to when things got tough. It was the only thing I knew how to do, even as a child: be a caretaker, a peacemaker. Keep the peace no matter what. Try harder to make everyone happy. Stay positive. None of it was working.

All I wanted was for this journey to go smoothly. I wanted to make a family.

This time I heard them say the words to me and I had to believe them, even though it was so unbelievable to me. But wait, only Jackie said it. Maybe there was hope for Michael? It was all starting to sink in but so many pieces were missing. I kept denying it was true.

The strategies I used all my life to hold myself together were slowly crumbling. I could feel little pieces falling away inside. I was a woman before I became a mother, and when I became a mother I started to see myself as only a mother to my boys. I lost myself somewhere along the way and realized that I never knew myself at all. I started asking real questions like, who am I?

Being a surrogate mother only complicated all of it.

We lived in the South Bay of Los Angeles in a little beach town I adored but could barely afford. I moved my boys, Brian and Steven, who were both in elementary school, two years ago after an ugly divorce from their father. After numerous attempts at a regular, full-time job as an administrative assistant failed due to childcare issues, I applied for my daycare license so I could support my family financially and be home for the boys.

I asked a good friend of mine who was in between roommates herself, Theresa, if she needed a roommate. We'd been friends since childhood and we were roommates years before when we were in college. It seemed only fitting to share the rent of a cute little three-bedroom house with someone I could trust with my kids, probably the only one I trusted, so we could both afford to live in a beautiful town with great public schools for the boys.

I walked in Brian and Steven's room that morning and saw them snuggled up into their beds with comfy blankets. I gave a light tug at the bottom of their twin bed covers. "Time to get up, guys, let's go. School time." They both barely budged.

I made my way up the stairs to the kitchen and found a small glass of orange juice in the refrigerator I'd left from yesterday. I downed it and headed to the television to turn on cartoons for the boys. As I flipped on the television, the twins started kicking together; all morning they felt a little more restless than usual. Both were vying for the top space near my ribs. They jabbed me from the left, right, front, and back. Little fingers reached around both sides. I smiled because I loved feeling life move within me. There is a certain double-life pregnancy magic with twins, feeling two sets of hands with twenty fingers, feet with twenty toes, two sets of arms and legs.

Theresa walked into the kitchen while I was planted in front of the television in the living room.

"Morning," she said and started making coffee.

I didn't answer right away, trying to make sense of what I was seeing on the television. I saw a tall building on fire. All of a sudden, I watched a plane hit a second building. *What is this? Is this happening?* Shocked that it might be real, I turned the channel to find coverage on every single station. It was real. I looked over at Theresa as she walked into the living room. I looked at her with my eyebrows up, not knowing exactly what to say.

"What's going on, Suz?" she asked as she glanced over at the television. Dark plumes of smoke were rising from one of the towers. I heard a reporter say, "We have word the twin towers may have been struck with U.S. airplanes by terrorists." The bottom headline caption framed the television, "WORLD TRADE CENTER DISASTER."

"It's, um, I'm not sure," I said, my voice trembling with more fear and shock. I tried to catch my breath and not cry. We both sat fixated on the television with few words. "Oh, my God. I can't believe this," Theresa said.

Tears started to fall down both our cheeks as we hunched together on the small white ottoman. It occurred to me that I didn't even have a chance to tell Theresa about the twins. And now this.

Brian and Steven still hadn't gotten up. All I could think of was trying to protect my own children from the wrongs of the world, but knew I couldn't. I wanted to protect what childhood innocence they had left, but it was impossible. It was a school day and they had to go to school. What would it be like there? What would the teachers say? I'll never forget their faces as they watched some of the coverage of 9/11 that morning. Concern, fear of the unknown, and all they don't know, all we didn't know. This was the day I would have to tell my boys some of the hard truths of the world, that it is unsafe sometimes and you have to be careful, but not so careful you live your life in fear.

Later that afternoon, I decided to call Michael. I needed clarification and to hear him say he really didn't want the twins. I already knew Jackie didn't because she made it very clear, but

Michael had faltered. I never heard him say it. I was getting ready to pick up the boys from school and my four after school daycare kids. Coverage of 9/11 was all over the news. I called him with my already trembling voice thinking he was going to confirm he didn't want the twins. This way at least I'd know more than I know now. He picked up on the first ring but didn't answer. I heard a muffled sound on the line.

"Michael?" No answer.

"Michael, I need to know. I need to know if you want the twins. I know Jackie doesn't, but please tell me what you want."

"Just quit bothering me, okay? There are bigger things right now. Terrorists destroyed the twin towers today," he said. He repeated the same sentence with scattered words. It sounded like he was crying. I could barely hear him and pulled the phone closer to my ear to hear him say it.

His voice was low, groggy, and desperately sad. "Stop," he said between deep heaving sobs. "I can't even take care of myself."

Click.

Barely thirty seconds into our conversation, the line went dead, and I felt instantly numb.

2

Becoming A Mother

My journey as a surrogate mother didn't begin the day I started the process with an agency in February 1999. My first real, conscious thought of becoming a surrogate began the day I gave birth to my first child in November 1989.

The morning air was crisp and the sun a bright ball of warm energy. I was on my way to the hospital to give birth to my first child. All I could think of was there is no turning back now. It's time.

I crunched a few leaves underfoot as my mother, and then-husband, Robert supported each of my arms as they walked me through a concrete walkway leading to the hospital. At the peak of a contraction, I felt my legs let go. I fell into my mom and Robert somehow grabbed me before I fell to the concrete. I was all baby, and it looked like someone had stuffed a big huge beach ball under my shirt. I saw a wheelchair a few feet away and didn't know how I was going to get there. The wheelchair made its way to me. After a few hard contractions I remember thinking, *when is this going to end?*

I was twenty-nine when I gave birth to our first child, a beautiful healthy baby boy. Brian was born in a large, busy hospital a mile from the ocean in Long Beach, California. Our newborn little boy had a dash of blondish golden hair, dark blue love-me eyes, and a hungry gene that made him famished from the moment he was born. He was frustrated with breast-feeding and screamed for more food. I compensated by giving him formula and my breast with hopes he'd want it after my breasts started producing more milk.

I laugh now when I recall that I brought a pretty, feminine white cotton maternity nightgown to wear after my baby was born. The cotton was light and airy with lacy trim. I had read all about it in an expectant mother's book. The hope was to instill the cozy warm feelings of home into my hospital room with natural relaxation to help induce breastfeeding. Although it felt more like home in my nightgown, I wished breastfeeding came more naturally for me, but I kept trying.

The advice in the expectant mother's book didn't warn me, though, that in the real world I would have to wear sanitary pads the size of adult diapers after delivery with huge panties, and it definitely did not tell me about all the blood that would come out of my body—and there was a lot of it. I had to change my pretty white nighty after about six hours because it wasn't so white anymore.

As I became more familiar with being a new mother, I watched my husband, Robert, call everyone we knew to announce our new arrival, who was born on his due date in November. We didn't find out the gender of the baby while I was pregnant, so we were able to share the joy of the surprise with our friends and family.

"It's a boy!" Robert said proudly over and over again. His tight blonde Afro ringlets curled down around his ear as he spoke on the phone. He was a proud daddy the fifth of five children, and our son was the first grandson in a family of five granddaughters.

He joined me by the bedside in between phone calls to gaze at Brian. I believe he loved every moment of being a new parent like I did.

"Wouldn't it be amazing for me to help another woman

have a baby?" I said to Robert.

Startled, he looked at me and said, "What? Are you out of your mind?" Apparently, my timing was never really on target in my conversations with Robert.

I moved up in the hospital bed holding Brian close to my breast. I nuzzled his little newborn head with my cheek, breathing in happiness. I admired the miracle we made and that I grew in my body. His newborn coos and baby sounds filled my ears.

"No, not really. I just thought of how wonderful it would be to carry a baby for someone who can't experience the unbelievable love and joy I'm feeling right now." He looked at me, puzzled. I'm sure he was thinking I might be a little bit crazy.

"No, Susan, that's gross and weird thinking of you carrying another man's baby," Robert said. His eye color often revealed his mood, ranging from sky blue to rigid steel blue, and they were steel showing his distaste for the subject.

"Plus, we have to have our own family first."

He added the last line for my benefit because he knew I was serious. I was drawn to things people didn't typically approve of, like surrogacy. I had no idea how the thought came to me, or where it came from, but I was reeling in the love and joy of being a new mother. It was exciting for me because I saw the beauty in it, especially when I thought about actually doing it.

"Why can't you open your mind even a little bit? I think it'd be so wonderful," I said.

"Let's think about our own family first." He frowned and moved away from the bed.

I watched Robert walk over to the window and back to the phone and thought maybe he was right. We needed to think of our family first. I felt like I was ruining our moment as a new family, and immediately knew it was something he probably wouldn't support.

But, it was something I thought would be an amazing thing to do. My thoughts went to the scores of women who could not have children. Although I knew nothing about surrogacy, I knew it was possible to have a child for someone who couldn't have one. I couldn't imagine having lived without being able to have had children. I appreciated those who chose not to have children, but for those who wanted to but couldn't, I felt a deep sense of sorrow and compassion for their loss.

I'd always wanted to do something huge with my life and make it matter. Helping someone make a family was the biggest thing I could think of. It would be an extraordinary gift. I imagined trusting a stranger to carry your biological child would be a huge endeavor. But when it's your only way to have a biological child, it seems one might find a way. I'd find a way if it were me. Then I pictured myself doing the hardest thing imaginable, handing over a baby I carried for someone else at birth. I pictured handing over my own baby and knew I couldn't do it. But with a baby that was not biologically related to me, I knew I could do it.

The miracle of Brian's birth overwhelmed me. After the last hard push, I watched him come into the world. Every facial expression he made was etched into my memory, even now. My mouth opened when his did, as if to breathe his first breath with him. Wonder and awe filled my mind. He naturally responded by wailing out loud and long. His lungs filled the room with beautiful life music, crying with his little arms and legs reaching out and kicking. The doctor immediately put him on my belly straight from my warm body. My arms reached out with a fervent desire to hold him. I immediately peeled off my hospital gown and held him close to my skin, bringing him up to my breast. I was in love, and tears of unbelievable joy rolled down my cheeks. The happiness I felt was almost unspeakable. Becoming a mother brought me the greatest gift I could have ever asked for. Finding unconditional love was something I didn't expect, and no one told me about, something I'd always wanted to give and receive. Brian was someone who was a part of me and needed me.

I enjoyed my pregnancy. No wait, scratch that, I *loved* being pregnant and glowed the whole time with the fifty-pound weight gain. Some people told me I had to eat for two, which was a big fat lie. No one needs to eat that much. I didn't know what to expect with birth, but like any *firsts* everything was new. My labor lasted eight hours, and I was given an epidural for pain way too late in the labor. It didn't wear off fast enough, so I pushed hard and long for two hours not knowing how hard I was pushing because I couldn't feel it. My doctor said it resulted in "mountains of hemorrhoids." No matter how hard I pushed at 10 cm, Brian was not coming out anytime soon. I was given an episiotomy to get all 8 lb., 14 oz, and 22 inches out of my body. I was stretched beyond belief from the inside out. I saw Robert's face cringe when he watched the doctor make the cut from one end of my body to the next to pull our son out. Brian and I worked hard at labor and both ended up with fevers. I was shaking and shivering so hard after birth from the fever and tried to vomit, but nothing came out. So much for the natural birth I hoped for. More importantly, I wondered when I would walk again or sit down, let alone return to normal in my vaginal area. My doctor patiently stitched and weaved the pieces back together for over an hour, but I knew it would never be the same, and neither would my life.

Yet, in spite of it all, I was the happiest I'd ever been in my life. My connection to my baby was there the moment I found out I was pregnant, and intensified when I saw his sweet face and held him in my arms. I marveled in the wonder and miracle of birth. Something changed in me after he was born and I became a mother. I felt like I wanted to share that feeling I had with another woman whose own body had rejected her. At this point in time, surrogacy was almost unheard of. I'm not sure how this desire originated, but I wanted to share this special love and joy to help another woman become a mother.

By the time we left the hospital we were a new family of three. Even though I started to focus on my own new family, surrogacy was always in the back of my mind.

My world changed that day and not just a little. It was a

tectonic shift and I had a new purpose in life, to be a mother. It was a never-ending love, the kind I would die for.

A few years later, when Brian was almost two years old, I was approached for the first time about surrogacy at the UPS office while I shipped a package.

I scooped Brian up to do our errands and kissed his cheek multiple times. He giggled, and his little head full of blonde curls bounced across his forehead.

The lady behind the counter at the UPS store stuck out because she was unusually short. I'd seen her for a number of years before when I'd come in to ship packages for work. We weren't on a first name basis but she was so easy to remember because when she stood behind the high counter, I could barely see the top of her soft, manicured gray hair. I put my package on the counter, and she climbed onto her step stool to greet me.

"How's that cutie pie today?" she asked, looking at Brian in his stroller.

"He's good, just getting over a cold," I said and looked over at him and smiled.

"Awww, the wonders of children. Always something when they're little, ya know? Have you ever seen such a gorgeous day?"

I smiled and nodded, looking at Brian and then at her.

"Yes, pretty day," I said. I remembered that I never thanked her personally before for helping me because I never knew her name. I noticed she didn't have a nametag on.

She folded down a corner of her lip with her teeth and asked, "Have you ever heard of surrogacy?"

I hesitated and looked curiously at her. I didn't want to tell her that I'd thought about it after Brian was born, because I have a way of saying too much sometimes and get myself into things I can't get out of.

"I have, but don't know much about it," I said, wondering

what she was thinking.

"Aw, you look like you'd be a great surrogate mother," she said as she weighed my box. "My daughter and her husband are struggling to have a child, and it's killing me that she can't have a wee one."

She pulled new tape over my package. "They're ready to find a helper now, you know, a surrogate mother. Doc says they need help. Nothin' but disappointment and heartache, you know?"

She hopped off the step stool to bring the package to the back counter, turned, and sighed. "Do you know they've done IVF 11 times?"

"Oh wow, that's awful," I said with a soft voice, remembering how easy it was for me to get pregnant with Brian.

Without hesitating she said, "I don't imagine you would be interested in helping us, um, be a surrogate mother, would you?"

The early morning sun came through the window, making me squint.

A flash went through my mind of what it might be like, how happy it would make another person, but knew I'd say no feeling strange that I was caught off guard. Plus, there was no way Robert would agree to it. I thought about the comment he made about carrying another man's baby. I wasn't ready to commit to such a huge thing. Quite frankly, it scared the hell out of me because the possibility of it just became real.

I politely told her I was three months pregnant with our second baby. She looked surprised at first and then smiled like she was happy for us.

I wanted to say I'd help her daughter later but didn't want to commit myself and give them false hope. I knew I couldn't and wouldn't follow through. The thought started to scare me. Why did I think it was something I should do? Or why did I think I owed her any explanation? The thought of it all surprised me. I wondered how much or how long you should know someone before you become their surrogate. There wasn't much chance of me becoming a surrogate for them.

"Well, I'm sure you'll find someone to help," I said.

"Yep, I'm asking those women who I see have babies, one or two, who might be interested because you just never know."

I felt her eyes follow us to the door as we left the store. I looked back to wave goodbye.

Six months later, in July 1992 Brian and I were at the mall to escape the sweltering heat. We spent hours there until it cooled down outside. I also needed to buy him some new clothes because he was quickly growing out of everything. Hugely pregnant with our second baby, I could barely waddle anywhere fast.

A nice-looking, professionally dressed couple walked by us and peered over at Brian in his stroller. I stopped because Brian was holding up a treasured leaf he found on the ground. He held it up as they walked by, offering it to the pretty woman dressed in a frilly lavender dress. She stopped in front of the stroller, struck by his generosity.

"Oh, thank you. This is the most beautiful leaf I've ever seen," she said and pushed back her bouncy brunette curls. She bent down onto her knees in front of him. She twirled the leaf with her fingers in front of his eyes. "Thank you," she said warmly and touched him the top of his head.

Such a sweet gesture, I thought. She stood up, tousling Brian's hair. He jumped up and down in his stroller. I noticed tears welling in the woman's eyes.

She glanced at my very pregnant belly and said, "You are so lucky." She emphasized the word *so*. I knew what she meant.

After a long moment of silence, Brian screamed with joy and pointed at lights near the Disney Store, jumping up and down in his stroller with excitement.

She started to sob and put her hand over her mouth and buried her head into her husband's chest. I was touched and didn't know what to say. She moved from him and turned to quickly walk away. I heard her say, "I'm sorry, I…" She couldn't finish her sentence and hurried away. Her cry followed her.

Her husband stayed a moment longer. He said in a loud whisper, "We got another negative pregnancy test this morning with our last IVF attempt. It's been seven years, and the one thing she wants most in the world, I can't give her."

He managed a smile and then went after his wife.

I'd never wanted something more than I wanted a baby for that woman. A woman I didn't know. I felt her pain and wanted to help her in some way.

The following month, we were blessed with another healthy, beautiful son named Steven. My second birth was easier than the first and just as magical for me as a mother. I loved being a mother and my life felt full with a new baby and a toddler. Even though I wanted to have more children in the future, the two we had were a handful and kept me busy. But something within me was still missing. I didn't know what it was or how to fix it, but it was there just underneath the surface. I started questioning everything.

I started asking myself if I wanted to stay married to Robert. Did I love him? Did I want more kids with him? Unresolved feelings of shame and lack of self-worth I buried years ago with our relationship were starting to resurface. I tried to suppress the bad feelings, push them down deeper like I did as a child, but it wasn't working anymore. I couldn't deny the truth any longer. It was being uprooted naturally. The more I stood up for myself about anything, the stronger I felt. I wanted to let go of the bad stuff, but I didn't know how. Underneath it all was what I feared the most. Anger. The anger I felt was fierce, so strong it vibrated deep inside.

I always tried so hard to be the strong one, the good girl like I did when I was a child. All of that was starting to go to hell. I started to stand up for myself when I felt strongly about something, anything, and it was creating more strain on our marriage.

Later that year I thought about talking to Robert again about surrogacy. I got as far as thinking I would demand that he let me be a surrogate. Then I thought of how stupid that statement was. Why would I have to get his approval for something I wanted to do? Why couldn't we support each other as individuals with our wants and our needs? That wasn't the only thing. There were a lot of other things we didn't agree on, and he would always have the deciding vote.

I felt a desire to be pregnant again and wanted another child, but I would not bring another child into our relationship. I knew another child would only create more problems than we already had.

We didn't have a perfect or even good relationship, but I kept pretending we did.

3

End of A Marriage

Ten years into my marriage I knew it was over. It was a cold, wet February evening in 1996, one day before Valentines Day. I waited for Robert to show up for an appointment at our marriage and family therapy office, but somehow I knew he wasn't coming.

While Robert was a good dad to our boys, I didn't want to be married to him anymore.

I wasn't sure what exactly changed in our relationship, but I knew I was changing. I felt like I needed something more as a woman. I was emotionally moving away from my husband, and the space between us felt large and ominous. The worst part of our relationship was that I could feel myself falling out of love with him. It was something I couldn't deny. I was done with his excessive drinking and smoking pot. We used to do this together when we were dating, but I stopped just before we got married. Even worse, I was sick of myself nagging him about it all the time. I was honest with him about how I felt and wanted him to say something to save us. Anything. Something. I nagged more to get a response. I was dying for him to say something to help us stay together, but he said nothing.

I desperately wanted our family to remain together, but

knew if I stayed it would be exactly the way it was for the rest of my life, and I simply couldn't do it. I pictured myself another ten years down the road and hated what I saw—a stifled, mean, and angry-hearted woman who should have quit her marriage years before to save herself.

I yearned for more and hungered for a different kind of love. It was an intimate kind of love. It was something I had no idea how to get, yet I could feel it, sense it, and wanted it desperately in a relationship.

I noticed how, in the past few years, I had changed when I started talking about my childhood sexual abuse at the hands of my stepfather. I told those closest to me about my abuse when I heard Oprah say on national television for the first time, "It's not your fault." I was shocked. For many years that was all I knew, it was my fault. Oprah is telling me it's not? She confessed her childhood sexual abuse on live television, and it stirred a secret buried deep inside of me. It was so deep I wasn't sure where it was. I thought to myself, *What? It's not my fault?* Her words had a huge impact on me and opened me up in ways I couldn't explain. That day Oprah became a mentor to me, and a voice for victims of child abuse all over the world. I tried to talk to Robert about my abuse as a child, but he didn't know what to do with the new information. It certainly wasn't his fault that he didn't know what to say or do, but he wouldn't talk about it at all. We drifted apart more and more as the days went on. While I felt it was very close to the end of our relationship, I had to make a good attempt at trying to save it before I lost all the love I had for him.

So on that cold, February day, I sat alone in a chair across from our marriage therapist with a box of tissues to my side feeling embarrassed. I was pretty sure I wouldn't need any because I was more angry than sad that Robert wasn't going to show up. He'd already told me he didn't want any therapy or marriage counseling and had only showed up a few times because I insisted.

The therapist had a calm demeanor and a finely chiseled

face framed with dark rimmed glasses. He was about thirty or so, and I towered over him when I first shook his hand. He sat in his chair across from me patiently waiting for Robert in an office that didn't show any personality. No pictures and nothing on the tables except for a light and a pad of paper with a pen. I thought maybe he shared it with other therapists.

"He's not coming," I said. This was my fifth visit and would have been Robert's third. He was supposed to come directly from work. I reminded him earlier and arranged for a babysitter for the kids.

Twenty-five minutes into our appointment, the therapist and I still waited, making small talk.

The therapist turned to me and said, "Maybe your marriage was over before it began, Susan."

I sat there and started to feel numb, staring straight ahead. Was that a question? I knew he was right, I just never heard it said that way before. I'll never forget those direct words. My marriage was over before it began ten years earlier. I looked out of the large portrait window and gazed at the tall green trees outside wondering why I was there alone. I never felt so alone as in that moment. Maybe I was the one who needed future therapy, not Robert. I looked back at the therapist and completely forgot what I was going to say. I'm sure I looked lost sitting on the big, soft brown leather couch. I stared at the tissue box swearing I wouldn't cry and took another minute to stare out the window to regain my composure. It helped me focus. He waited for me to talk. I heard what he said, but felt silenced, unable to talk about it at all. Why did I think it was such a big secret?

He was referring to what happened about one week before Robert and I married; Robert cheated on me at his bachelor party. It was all coming back into the open ten years later. I didn't regret marrying him, though, because I wouldn't have my two boys if I hadn't.

I managed to say, "Yeah, I know, but it's so hard." I thought about how I had lied to my husband *and* myself pretending to love everything he did. I wrapped myself into his world of sports even though I found it boring. I thought we were bonding, but I was really losing sight of myself, my own interests. It was clear to me he would never be able to give me the kind of love I craved, but it was my fault because I started to want different things in life. I was the one who changed, not Robert.

"How are you feeling about what I said?" The therapist pushed his glasses back on while he held his writing tablet with the other hand. I wondered if he was married and what other stuff I would have to answer. I knew I had made bad choices, and I felt myself getting defensive.

"I'm not sure, but I know it's true." I let out a nervous laugh. I looked at the therapist, but he said nothing.

My mouth started spilling the truth I had been holding onto for ten years.

"After Robert admitted he cheated, I had no time to process it all, let alone forgive him. I was beyond devastated and never cried like I did the night I found out. A little part of me died that night. It was three days before our huge three-hundred-guests wedding in a big Catholic church. The reception was planned and paid for by us aboard *The Queen Mary.* After we talked, I cried for days about it all. Then, I did the unthinkable. I told him I would never bring it up again because I loved him."

I sighed and looked out the window. "How stupid was that?" I added. "But I wanted to marry him anyway. I knew I would either marry him or walk away and never see him again." The taste in my mouth was bitter when I admitted it out loud. My memory brought me back to that feeling I had ten years ago of my world falling apart.

The therapist gave me an empty look like I needed to answer my own question. Dammit, that frustrated me. *What was the answer?* I cleared my throat.

"I won't lie about being shocked that it happened to me," I said. Then I kept thinking, *what did I do wrong? Why?*

I went on to tell him that I kept my promise to Robert and

never brought up the cheating to him again for ten long years, and I had no idea why. The hurt behind the action came back.

"I let it simmer way down deep, like a big fat obstacle to any good we might have had in our relationship." My voice fell into a sob, but I kept talking.

"Through those years, I never forgot how my wedding day was not the happiest day of my life. It was probably one of the saddest. I remembered thinking so hard how I wished I'd never found out about the bachelor party and wondered if things might have been different."

"Do you think it would have been different?" he asked.

"Probably not, but now even after all of that, all I could think was, is this the kind of love that I want for the rest of my life with this man." It wasn't. But my thoughts at the time were all about me, and wondering why I wasn't enough? I thought it was something I didn't give him. I wanted to be enough for him at that time, but what I didn't know was that it had nothing to do with me.

I grabbed a few tissues from the box sitting next to me. Sometimes it felt like Robert and I were strangers, or like brother and sister sleeping in the same bed, existing in life, not living it.

"I've gone over it so many times in my head, and I know that kind of intimate love I'm looking for is possible, soulful, and mature. I can't change what happened before our marriage, but I know it's time for me to move on. It's just hard to make the first move."

"Do you want to divorce Robert?" he asked as he grabbed another pad of paper.

"Yes, but I don't know how to. I don't want to hurt him or break up our family." I really wanted the best of both worlds but knew it would be impossible.

"Sometimes you have to do what is best for you," he said.

It all sounded so foreign to me. The thought struck me and I went deeper to reveal a personal thought. "I've always had revenge on my mind. Does that make me a bad person?"

He studied me and tilted his head to one side. "I wouldn't say that it makes you a bad person. It makes you human."

"I don't want to be in an unhappy marriage, and I don't want to keep making the same mistakes with men." I trembled at the thought of being alone with two small children, but most of all, I didn't want to end up like my mother—married and divorced five times.

"Then take your time, Susan. Get to know who you are before you jump into a relationship," he said.

I left his office knowing I had to end my marriage, but I didn't know how to do it. I thought we'd be married forever and this was a big thing for me. The thought of confronting Robert with it made me ill. The next year of our marriage was incredibly unhappy for both of us. I was dying to get out but had zero courage to end it. One evening we had a big argument and I told him I was going to file for divorce the next day. I'm not sure he believed me but I ended up filing the very next day.

The truth was I didn't know how to be married, but there was no box on the form to check for that. The only open box that applied was irreconcilable differences.

I was a perfectionist and a control freak. Add fiercely independent in with it and that would be an ideal description of me. And, I'm sure Robert would say I wasn't an easy person to be married to.

He grew furious after I filed, worse than I'd ever seen him. Sometimes I felt his anger turn into fear in my mind, and it made me wonder if I really ever knew him at all. I asked that he not drink alcohol when he was with the boys, but he insisted on doing what he wanted. He was clearly unhappy and wouldn't work with me.

Our divorce didn't go like I hoped. I fantasized we would talk everything out like grown-ups and work out our disagreements about child support arrangements, but it didn't work out that way. He wouldn't even agree to the divorce. It took years, and thousands of dollars I didn't have along with many visits to the courthouse before it was finalized. I ran out of money to pay my attorney before I was even divorced. Many years later, I would learn through more therapy that Robert's premarital infidelity had nothing to do with me, and everything to do with him. This was something I wish I'd known before I married him. It seems like it might have saved me a lot of hurt to know it, but it's one of those things in your life that you don't know until you do.

By the end of our marriage, any relationship we had left was fueled with financial disaster, accusations, hurt feelings, and broken hearts with two little boys sandwiched in between.

4

A New Start

By the end of 1998, I was a thirty-seven-year-old single mother with two young boys. Brian, who was almost nine years old, had blond hair and an amazing, tender heart. As the oldest, he excelled with the first-born traits you read about. Steven, who was six years old and a natural towhead, had an uncanny ability to befriend strangers and was naturally drawn to fear nothing. He had easy confidence and the bluest eyes you've ever seen. Both of them shared so many qualities, yet they were so different. They shared Robert's supernatural ability to remember names, faces, and statistics, especially if it was sports related.

After the divorce, my plan was to move to a quiet, affluent beach town about thirty minutes south of Los Angeles. I had a computer software sales job at the time, but my plan to live in this town would only work if I had a roommate to share the rent.

I had been talking to a good, long-time friend of mine about being roommates. Theresa and I met in junior high after my mother divorced for the third time in 1974. My mom moved us back to south Oceanside, California where we lived before she married my stepfather, Donald. Theresa and I were barely teenagers, and after we met, we acted more like sisters than most sisters.

The craziest moment of our friendship was the day Theresa and I found out we knew each other long before we met in junior high school. It was when she helped me move into our new apartment in 1981 while we were preparing to go to college. She grabbed a framed picture of mine off the top of a box as I carried it into our new place.

"Hey, why do you have my kindergarten picture?" she said.

I turned around to see what she was talking about.

"No, it's mine," I said. "I'm right here." I pointed to a tall, frowning pixie-cut, tow-headed five-year old girl in the top row.

"I'm here!" she said, laughing as she pointed to a poised and smiling little girl with shoulder length blonde hair with a big navy bow in her hair.

"Oh, my God, we were in the same kindergarten class!" we said at the same time. We laughed until we ached staring at the picture together and at the uncanny moment of finding out we were in the same kindergarten class in south Oceanside.

Theresa was now at a point in her life where she needed a roommate too.

"Can you believe we are going to be roommates again after seventeen years?" she said.

But this time, it wasn't just the two of us. Now it included my boys, our lab/retriever, Boomer and Theresa and her big black dog mix, Bear. He was her baby. She wasn't married and didn't have children. We searched and searched for a house that would work for all of us. We found it was much harder to find a house to rent that accepted dogs, let alone two kids, and one almost divorced single mom with bad credit resulting from her pending divorce. Luckily, Theresa carried us on her good credit, and I carried us with the promise of fixing up the house and keeping it nice. Theresa knew the housing market and mentioned to me that we'd have to go back several times to the house we are interested in because there were so many people looking for housing.

"The dogs won't be a problem," we promised the owner as we waited for his answer after the third time visiting the house.

"Well, okay," he said hesitating to give us verbal approval.

"Five others fell through, so I guess it's meant to be that you rent the place," he said.

The cute little three-bedroom, two-bath house with a beige exterior and blue trim was waiting for us directly across from an award-winning elementary school for the boys. It couldn't have been a better choice for us.

As Theresa, the kids, and I all adjusted to the new house and living together, we found ourselves falling into a routine. The boys were settling somewhat and making new friends. They seemed to like their new school.

Robert and I finally agreed on joint custody. He was scheduled to see the boys once a week on Wednesday evenings and every other weekend. He rarely followed our agreed-upon schedule, though. He focused more on the boys' sports calendar than anything and would see them during their baseball practice after school a few times a week and skipped the weekend stay-overs. I hoped the boys would have their own relationship with him, in their own way, as they grew up. Robert lived thirty minutes away.

I made an appointment with a child psychologist to see how the boys were dealing with the divorce. The psychologist took out a book and read it, personalizing the divorce for them. I bawled the whole time in the background while the boys listened to the story, and what divorce means as a family breaks up. Every once in a while a set of blue eyes would look back at me. I often heard the term "broken home" when I was talking to others about divorce and many used it as a label. I resented it because I knew many homes that were fractured, shattered, and broken where there was no divorce.

A few months later, I found an essay Brian wrote at school in which he internalized everything and thought it was his duty to be the man of the house. It broke my heart because I never wanted him to feel that way, to assume any responsibility. I guessed it might have come from Robert.

He often said to me, "I don't want to grow up, Mommy." It was as if he sensed the drudgery of being an adult when he was so young.

Steven followed with the wish of having more siblings. "I'm sad we aren't a family anymore," he said. "I want a sister or brother to play with."

Although I wanted more children, it wasn't in my immediate future.

Through the hurt, confusion, and angry, hurtful moments, I vowed to stay single once I got divorced. I swore I'd never marry again.

5

Falling into Gray

Months after the start of my divorce early on before surrogacy in 1997, I didn't waste any time starting new flings with any man who took a second look at me, but I had no intentions to settle down.

There was only one man throughout the time I was single that I brought home to meet the boys. Douglas and I had been dating for about six months. He was a tall, gentle, kind-hearted person. He was the kind of guy my mother loved and she never stopped telling me, "You are so lucky to have found such a wonderful man, Susan."

That was my mom: Give all the credit to the man, and make sure I knew how lucky I was to have found him. I admit he seemed like a great guy and an excellent catch. He adored the boys and they him. He cooked often and made better chocolate chip cookies than I did. On top of that, he was successful in the IT field of computer-generated graphic artwork. You might think I'd be grateful for meeting such a sweet, loving man, but I didn't know what to do with him. I wasn't ready. He told me he loved me, but I couldn't return his love. Douglas and I lasted eight months because I didn't love him, and I didn't trust him. It wasn't his fault, though, because I didn't trust any man.

After Douglas, moving on with a new relationship felt impossible. I came to the realization that I was still hopelessly in love with a married man who I had a short affair with just after my separation from Robert.

I knew I needed time alone to get to know myself. Although, I admit, I acted quite the opposite and held onto anything that resembled a relationship. But I always dropped every single relationship when I felt trapped, which was always. Any meaningful relationships felt forbidden because I was afraid to end up married again. I still gravitated toward the *bad boy type* with younger men, some twelve to fifteen years younger than I was, and wound up in one-night stands drinking the nights away while I worried about the boys, who were with their father once in a while for the weekend. Most of the encounters weren't even one night. The bad boys were the ones that didn't want the relationship either. Some lasted an hour, making out passionately with men I didn't know in upscale restaurants, restroom stalls, in one of our cars, and many more having no idea where I was, or who I was with, just to feel the touch of another person and remember I was human.

The guilt I felt about breaking up my marriage was huge. And even though I didn't want to, I knew there was no going back to my old life.

Before I put the brakes on love and relationships, I went the one place I knew I shouldn't go—back to the married man.

We met online in the early days of the first social media internet giant, AOL (American On-Line) in late 1997 where they charged a fee for their monthly service. This experience took me back to a place I loved, writing.

This man emailed me after we talked in a private forum with twelve other people, all men. I was the only woman that I knew of. We wrote to each other at length, sharing our deepest, most inner thoughts online with sexual scenarios showing voyeuristically how the scenes fit in with our own personal fantasies. We decided early on not to meet or share photos, which created a safety net for our intimate cyber friendship. Photos back then were not as easy to share like they are today. This experience let me be open and honest with anonymity. Our conversations were exciting and I was always learning something new. I could express whatever I wanted without being called out. I was hungry to see how men operated and explore how different they were from women. Most of all, I wanted to know their secrets.

I developed a fondness for this man whose online personality was deeper and more meaningful than those who just wanted to meet and get into your panties as soon as possible. He wrote a short essay to me about himself and was curious about me. I wrote back and started to get to know him. I got a feel for his hesitant or excited keystrokes when he entered text during live prompts, or by the endless stories of sexual fantasy, poetry, and personal letters we wrote to each other imagining who each other could be. We wrote hundreds of stories to each other. He wrote beautiful stories to me. It was something I was not used to from men.

After a few months going back and forth with him, it woke up the literary me and rekindled my childhood love for writing stories, plays, and poetry.

Back in third grade, I won a small trophy for talent in a play I wrote and acted out a 1969 talent show. I stopped writing the next year after a teacher wrote in red ink at the top of one of my creative stories, "Writing is not your forte." Along with the comment was a big fat "F" in the middle of the paper. I didn't know what she meant by forte, and she wouldn't explain it to me.

When I got home from school, I took the dictionary into my closet and hid my paper at the bottom of all the discarded clothes. I looked up the word and still didn't know what it meant, but knew it wasn't good. I found two empty vodka bottles there that my mother must have tried to hide. Instead of hiding them like I usually did, I shut the closet door and cried hard, wiping my snot all over the clothes.

Weeks later, after I'd forgotten about the paper, my step-father, Donald, found my paper on the floor of the room I shared with my sister. I cringed when I saw him pick it up and glance at the paper, and then I watched him laugh out loud. He laughed as loud as he yelled, and his laughter was never about something funny.

"You aren't worth a damn, Susan," he said in between his laughter. "You'll never amount to anything, so don't even try." He crumpled up my story into a tiny ball and threw it across the room. Suddenly, I didn't feel anything like my stories. In the stories I created, I felt big and strong, like a superhero creating a world from nothing. He shot it down with one sentence and a condescending laugh without knowing the story at all. His action made me feel that my voice didn't matter. I grew more silent and felt smaller taking up less space in the world.

Back in the adult online world, this new man encouraged my writing and was incredibly supportive for someone I'd never met in person. I started to like him more, and some of my stories became more creative when he typed back to me, "I love your stories, Susan, and I longingly wait for them every day."

Really? I thought. I wasn't the best writer in the world and I made a lot of mistakes. I opened up to him more than I ever did with any man, and the only personal information we shared were our first names, married or not, and whether we had kids.

His name was Adam, and he was married with two kids. I was married too, with two kids, but heading for a divorce.

Eventually, we talked on the phone. I was against it at first because I didn't want our cyber friendship to go any further, but he said he didn't want to be talking to some supposed *girl* that turned out to be a guy getting his kicks out of screwing him over online. It sounded fair enough to me, and I wondered if I could fall for a man I had never met in person.

Months went by as we talked on the phone. We continued to write stories to each other. One day after I wrote him a particularly heartfelt story he said to me, "You make words feel."

It was poetry to my heart and brought up new energy I'd never felt with another person. It made me feel alive. I thought of what he said over and over again. *I can make words feel?* Could I be that naive? Was I living in a fairytale fantasyland? *Was he who he said he was?* I wrote what he said in my journal anyway so I could remember it. The simple fact that I could possibly make someone feel my words was exciting.

I loved asking and discovering the intimate secrets of men. We could ask each other anything. Nothing was off limits. We confessed things to each other that blew my mind. Things I always wanted to know like, "Where do men masturbate the most?" Without hesitation, he typed, "In the shower." He shared with me the most private details about himself growing up with his younger sister.

He said, "We'd play sexual games that my single mother knew nothing about, and they would arouse me as a young man. Although we never fucked, it was as close as anyone gets. As we grew up and became adults, we never spoke to each other about our secrets as children. In fact, you are the first person I've ever told."

"Do you think about it now?" I typed. "In fantasy?"

"Every now and then," he admitted.

It felt like I knew him better in six months than I did my ex-husband after ten years of marriage.

He mentioned he counseled others on hardships in their lives. I laughed out loud because I needed a counselor with all that was going on in my life. I shared with him that I'd like to be a surrogate mother one day. He told me it'd be a wonderful thing to do for another person. We talked endlessly about our kids, relationships, our souls, along with intimate talks pondering the universe and what we thought it meant to find real love. He said he loved his wife, and though I believed him, it didn't seem possible if he was sharing so much intimate time with me online.

"I can say more to you than I've ever said to my wife in all the years we've been married," he said many times.

I wondered where his marriage went wrong and knew where mine had. What kind of love did he think he had with his wife? When I asked, he said, "Getting the kind of love I'd like from my wife is like getting water from the moon."

I connected with his poetic language and wondered what we might be like together as a couple. I found myself wanting to kiss him. I had no idea what he looked like, so I imagined the man of my dreams that fit his voice on the phone. In my mind, he was tall, dark, and handsome.

Months later before a scheduled phone call, I realized I felt like I was falling for him. Our relationship was getting deeper and we were getting to know one another very well while keeping our identities secret. Ten minutes before our call, I printed out a scenario he wrote so I could read my favorite parts back to him over the phone.

The printout didn't look like it normally did. It was separated text throughout the page and didn't look like a regular paragraph of words. I looked closer and saw a last name on the second line, one I didn't recognize. I looked at the first name. It read Adam. I continued reading: Adam Redding, Southern Baptist Bible School, LA, CA, Pastor Adam Redding. It had a home address with a telephone number and area code in Los Angeles, CA.

I re-read, "*Pastor* Adam Redding."

I was gobsmacked.

I was both excited and shocked. Excited that I knew about him and he didn't know about me, and shocked that he was a pastor of a church and he was having an emotional affair with me. I wondered what church he worked at, what it looked like, and how many people he preached to. It brought a new twist to our relationship. I wondered if I should tell him or keep it to myself.

I paced wondering how long I could keep it a secret.

I imagined him at a pulpit preaching the word. After all the secrets we shared, it made him so human to me.

The telephone rang.

"He-llo," he said in his oh-so-sure way I came to think of as adorable. It always felt like he was totally delighted to speak with me. I could hear his chair squeaking in place as he leaned back to engage in our conversation. What did his office look like? Was he at the church now? What did he know as a pastor that I didn't know? I wondered if he had a closer connection to God than I did.

"Hello, Pastor Adam," I said knowing I couldn't keep it from him.

Silence.

I heard his chair squeak back upright and I wondered if this might destroy what we had online. It would definitely change things.

"Oh my God. How did you find out?"

"I printed out the story you wrote and the first page had your information on it," I explained. "It looks like a new bible software application that printed information back to a company or something like that."

"Well, that's the last time I put personal information into a computer application," he joked.

He typically used humor in tight situations.

I laughed. "I had to tell you. It showed where you live and that you are a pastor. I have to admit I was having fun being the one in charge with all the info."

He cleared his voice. "I guess this takes us to a different level, doesn't it?"

"I guess so, counselor."

"I do counsel my parishioners all the time," he said in a serious voice.

"Right," I said softly, all the while thinking there might have been some occasions that he officially counseled people, though I'm sure he listened and referred to books a lot.

"To make things right between us, I have to ask, you're not a nun, right?" He asked this with a serious voice, but then we both laughed.

"Nowhere close," I said. "Although, it might be fun to dress up as one."

"God, I love your sense of humor, Susan." His chair squeaked back into our conversation position. "Does it make things different between us?" he asked.

"Well, yeah, kind of. I mean, it feels weird to write sexual scenarios to a pastor." I thought about *The Thorn Birds*, one of my favorite books and movie. I could not picture myself as a pastor's wife, but it was like I was in competition with both God and his wife.

Without skipping a beat he said, "My wife put my AOL bill under my pillow last night and highlighted the amount I spent this month."

I laughed. "Oh, my God, really? I think I like her."

Through our conversations I discovered he was no ordinary counselor or therapist. He was the pastor of a very large church nearby. By this time we'd known each other online for almost nine months, and we'd had no intentions to meet, but we had both become curious. Within a few short weeks we decided to meet in a crowded restaurant in another city.

Decked out in a short red dress and red pumps, I scanned the busy lobby of the restaurant when I walked in. He told me he would be holding a red rose. I felt ridiculous when I didn't see a man with a rose. I wondered if I was too early or maybe he wasn't going to show up? I started back out the door and saw a man sitting behind the front door, holding a red rose and sporting a smile from ear to ear.

I approached him with the shyness of a schoolgirl, my long blonde hair swaying behind me. I am tall for a woman, and wearing heels put me at just about six feet. He stood and I noticed he was a few inches shorter than I was. He looked like you might imagine a pastor would: Stocky, medium build, mousy brown hair, glasses, and a sweet round face you could easily talk to. When we nervously hugged, his sweater lingered with the archaic smell of intriguing books and a slight hint of mothballs. I loved to smell books and guessed he must have come from his office. No doubt he had stacks of books like Bibles and religion or theology books throughout his office.

"You said you were tall, but really?" he said after we hugged.

I laughed. "I told you I wouldn't lie to you as long as you don't lie to me." I went to sit down and he reached over to pull my chair out, then he sat.

"So, here we are," he said and smiled as he nervously touched the top of his head to push his bangs back onto his head.

"Yes, so we are." I tilted my head down and smiled timidly because of all the secrets we shared. I thought of how transparent and vulnerable I was with him. I had told him everything.

As the late afternoon to early evening progressed, the world around us disappeared. I wasn't sure how I felt about him, but I knew it was something. We knew each other so well. He knew how I liked my coffee and that I hated cheese. He even knew what I fantasized about in bed late at night.

I had never given thought before to meeting him. Ever. I knew our relationship was wrong because we were both married. He knew all about my pending divorce and tried his best to talk me out of it. He preached to me to keep working on my marriage, but I wasn't open to his counseling.

I wasn't ready to kiss him that night, but he kissed me anyway. He waited until it was dark and walked me to my car. His kiss wasn't what I expected. It was messy, sloppy, and nervous. His stories and words were one thing, his kissing quite another. Did I really want to start something with this man? I was trying hard to find things I didn't like so it would be easier to run.

We continued to write to each other for another few months, and my love for his words won out, so we agreed to meet again. He invited me over to his house one night during the Christmas holiday when his wife and kids were away. It was risky and felt forbidden, but we were living in our stories and it added to the excitement.

Christmas was everywhere, and the letdown a day after was there too. It was strange walking into his house where he lived with his family. The homey smells once I hit the kitchen were unfamiliar. I set my purse down on one of the kitchen chairs. I looked around knowing I did not belong there. I should have turned around and left, but I didn't.

It was plain, like my own home, except for pictures of Jesus and crosses everywhere. Some rooms had two or three plaques of Jesus. *Oh God*, I thought. I didn't expect this. I was at a point in my life where I was questioning and doubting anything religious. He showed me around, and then we headed back to the living room. As we walked through the doorway, he pulled me to him up against the doorjamb, breathing heavy against my face, he grabbed both my arms pulling them up above my head as if in surrender, and then he pressed his body firmly up against me. The heat of his body and the pressure of his sexual hunger matched my own.

"You know the power of a single written word, don't you?" he said. My heart pounded. The desire I had for him stirred and peaked.

"Yes, but I also know the strength of our sexual body chemistry right at this moment." My breath skipped in excitement. "Ahhh, I recognize this," I whispered thinking of a scenario where he took me after slight resistance, then surrender.

"Mmmmmm, you smell so good," he said. We kissed and it was wet, messy and passionate. Both of our hands feeling their way through the newness of each other's bodies. I pulled his chin to mine to slow him down, to let him feel my kiss and follow my tongue. Kissing was something that could be learned I thought. I wondered about his other skills. On paper they were excellent, but in person they remained to be seen.

I pulled back. "I'm not sure about this." We looked at each other and songs I didn't know played low and soft from his speakers praising the Lord Jesus with a Hallelujah.

The only religious Hallelujah song I knew was Leonard Cohen's, and it played in my head. "*I heard there was a secret cord…*" It abruptly ended when he kissed me again, inching me over to his new blue couch where we made out like teenagers, exploring every inch of each other's bodies underneath our clothes. He pulled off my sweater and lifted it to his nose. I grabbed his gray sweater and tossed it to the floor. My red bra with lacy white trim and matching panties were left. He looked at me adoringly and said, "Red, my favorite color."

I heard his breath quicken as he lowered my bra straps one by one. He reached around to undo my bra and his head came down to see my nipples exposed. The sound of his lips devouring my breasts was our own music. One piece of clothing after another followed until we were naked, our bodies pressed together. My sexuality had finally hit its peak, and I was no longer hung up on sex like I'd been for so many years. I wanted to know and feel everything. His smooth hands felt their way up my long legs as he reached between them touching me with his fingers, and brought them to his tongue. Somehow I didn't realize how strong my desires were for him until that moment.

I noticed a piece of clothing was caught on the edge of the lampshade. It tilted to the edge of the small table near the couch. One small nudge and it would hit the floor.

He stopped. I sighed heavily, and we both sat back up on the couch. I asked him to change the music because it was distracting. He did and then noticed the lampshade. He pulled his sweater off it and brought it back up to the table. We looked at each other like strangers. I thought of suggesting we go to his bedroom but decided against it. He'd already given me the song and dance that his wife doesn't understand him, and how they hardly ever have sex. I wasn't about to enter his bedroom where she laid her head, and we were not going to be together, if he wasn't ready. I remembered the best compliment he gave about his wife. "My wife is an expert in puritanical ways."

She and I couldn't have been more opposite.

Did she like his kissing? Did they ever kiss? He admitted to them both being virgins before marriage, which I thought was cute.

He said many times, "The Grand Design is to be shared in marriage only." I had no idea what the Grand Design meant so I asked him. He told me that a man and a woman fitting together, making love or during sex was the best design God had ever invented and that you should only share it in marriage. It fit when he told me that he never drank alcohol or went to parties. Dancing was prohibited and they followed strict Baptist laws, yet there we were naked in each other's arms. The fact that he never danced saddened me. To me, any kind of dance was a part of life. It's a way of moving your body and feeling free. How could God not like that I wondered.

He gently took me by the shoulders and kissed me deeply. We were back in the same position on the couch kissing and touching, hot and heavy, breathing hard. It felt like we might be close to having sex. Just as that thought entered my mind, I opened my eyes and saw Jesus staring at me from the wall. I closed my eyes and moved to change position.

Every time we got close to having sex that night, he stopped. It must have been the whole "can't cross that boundary, but everything else is okay" line we talked about. I knew the guilt he felt, but not having sex probably made him feel better that he didn't cross that line.

Religion was such a crock.

I pushed one more time, but he stopped altogether, looking forlorn.

"Okay, I think it's time for me to go," I said.

"I'm sorry, I—"

"No, don't worry about it. It's for the best. We shouldn't be doing this anyway."

"Let me walk you out." He pulled up his jeans. I found my black stirrup pants then my black cashmere sweater and pulled it over my head. I grabbed my purse from the chair. He shyly pecked my cheek inside the house as I headed for the door.

This was not in any scenario we wrote to each other. This was real life and shit got in the way.

It didn't take more than a month, though, before we jumped into bed together at a motel, which included exploring each other completely and having uninhibited, wild sex. We acted out our crazy sexual and voyeuristic fantasies, such as having sex up against a car in broad daylight, in a crowded parking lot while I was wearing a dress, or on my large office desk while I was working part-time at the eye center. I recall the excitement intensified as we listened to the janitors hit the vacuum up against the unlocked door, knowing they might come in at any minute. He showed me his church office one day, and it was exactly how I imagined it to be. I saw the squeaky chair and thought of the many phone calls we shared. He invited me over to his lap on the chair, and we had sex on that too.

He had made a way into my heart and mind before he ever touched and entered my body.

I wasn't proud of my behavior. In fact, I was so embarrassed I never told anyone about Adam for many years. This affair let me be who I thought I wanted to be, or at least who I was in my own fantasies. Over time we got to know each other very well. We continued our affair for years off and on until I'd put a stop to it when I'd get mad at myself for becoming the other woman, the woman I loathed. My biggest mistake in this affair was falling in love with him.

I wondered if his wife ever saw or noticed a difference in him.

Adam told me he had no intention of divorcing his wife and strangely, I didn't want him to. It's hard to explain why, except having him when I wanted him was easier, and to me, safer than dating. I didn't want a real relationship and it was convenient to call him, or so I thought, until I sat by myself on all those lonely nights—Christmas, New Year's, or any other holiday that I had to share him with God and his wife. I could never just pick up the phone and call him, and later when we had cell phones, texting was off limits. The only way we contacted each other was through email or he would call when he was free.

During our discombobulated affair, I played all the stupid little games, like trying to make him jealous dating other men. But he never batted a jealous eye and listened with interest about my dating stories, which made me crazy. Sometimes when the affair got to be too much and when I wanted more, I'd call it off, perplexed at how he kept it together.

"How do you separate yourself from our affair?"

"I compartmentalize it."

"What do you mean?"

"In my brain. I am hardwired and want a sexual life. I don't have that at home. I have no regrets being with you, Susan."

He knew full well the sin he was making once we crossed the boundary line of no return. Our relationship was never black or white. We went somewhere gray.

6

The Infertility World

In early 1999 after I broke up with Adam yet again, Theresa—or Terrie as I called her—and I were adjusting to our new home life with the boys and the dogs. I wanted to tell her about Adam, but decided not to. It made me feel bad about myself as a person, as a woman. I hoped I wouldn't call him again, because I wanted it to be over with us. I'd think about him, about us, and I'd miss him. I would put him out of my mind and think about how our relationship made me feel bad about myself. I'd do it again and again in my mind. It was the only way to not feel weak, cave and call him.

I had come to love our cozy home where there was a nearby park and a lot of activities throughout the city for the boys and my day care kids.

One Saturday morning while the boys were watching cartoons, I laid on the couch to read the local beach newspaper. I stumbled on an ad for egg donors that caught my attention. Intrigued, I read on because I loved anything having to do with science on the cutting edge. The ad read: "We're looking to help another woman have a child, can you help?" The ad featured a human stick figure on one knee *begging* with arms up, hands clenched together above the head and hearts floating up from its head. It was a funky little logo and I questioned why they would make it beg.

Surrogacy came to my mind after seeing the ad, and I wondered if now, after all these years, I might be able to be a surrogate mother. What I knew about egg donation was that it helped women with egg issues have a child. It often went hand in hand with surrogacy, sometimes when a woman could not carry a child herself or had egg issues with her fertility, or both. I thought maybe I was too old to be an egg donor, so why would I call the number on the ad? But I felt compelled. Out of pure curiosity, I picked up the phone and found myself calling the number to join a group appointment for the next day.

I made it to the egg center, walked in the door, and looked around the office. I was overwhelmed by the many different scents; it smelled like the Nordstrom's perfume aisle at Christmas time. The office was warm and comfortable with tones of black, brown, tan, orange, and cream. Everything seemed so earthy, even the burning candles. It was exactly how I would design an office if I had my own business.

"Call us, honey, don't forget," a nicely dressed woman with black shiny shoulder length hair said to a young woman heading out the door. The young woman put her hand up in the air to signal she had heard the woman behind the desk. Halfway through the door, I noticed the woman walking out was one of the most gorgeous early twenty- something women I'd ever seen. She smelled like a valley of lavender as she walked past me.

I didn't smell like anything, absolutely nothing, and couldn't remember the last time I used perfume.

"Sorry," I said to one of the possible donors as I walked past. I felt clumsy as I stumbled over her bare suntanned, long legs for a place to sit in an open chair. All different skin tones and shades were represented and each was stunning in some special way. I wondered if they were smart too. Colorful eyes, lips, hair, and all of the visual genes you might want for your child with egg donation. Everyone checked each other out and when their eyes met, they'd glance away. Some even peeked over magazines, sizing each other up.

I felt old in my mom jeans and plain, white, cotton long-sleeve shirt, which wasn't so white. I'm pretty sure it had a little yellow stain of barf near the right shoulder from when the boys were little. My inner critical voice reminded me of the two red pimples I spotted on my face when I brushed my teeth that morning. I didn't see any acne on these women, and I was older! Years older.

These young women were dressed the way I did before I became someone's mother. In fact, I could be their mother! Holy crap. Thinking like a mother, because I was one, I wondered if their mothers knew they were donating their potential grandchildren? Did any one of them mention to their mother that they might want to donate their eggs, let alone actually plan or *do* it?

I couldn't believe I was thinking this and suddenly felt like a fake. The girls didn't need their mother's permission to give their eggs to a couple in need because all they had to be was over twenty-one.

Huge relief came over me that I had two boys, but hoped I'd be the kind of mother who would understand if my daughter wanted to donate her eggs to those who needed them.

"Girls, all of you please come with me," a voice said from behind an open door. A hand with a very large diamond ring on the ring finger motioned for everyone to follow. It looked like they knew who they were and I didn't feel compelled to follow because I wasn't one of them. I stayed in my seat with another woman who seemed lost in whatever she was reading.

I couldn't help but wonder about the idea of giving my eggs to a woman who had none, or who might need help to have a child. It fascinated me and I felt a flush of adrenaline when my ego thought about how someone might *want* my eggs, my biology. It was a little psychological high that my DNA would go on forever in a child, or children, and I would never know. I wondered if any "maybe babies" from my eggs might one day come to know my boys. A scary thought! I mean, it was possible if I donated my eggs that my boys might meet up one day with their half-sisters or marry them. The possibilities were endless.

This particular agency was set up as anonymous egg donation, which meant the parties would retain their privacy and not get to know or meet one another, which meant they might never know that meeting their half-sisters (or half-brothers) might be possible. I wasn't so sure I agreed with the anonymous part, but it was something to think about.

After the girls left, I noticed the artwork on the walls and black marble sculptures on the tabletops of faceless people dancing, and holding hands depicting the wonder of life, swirling around carefree.

I stood up and grabbed my no-designer purse to keep myself busy and moved from frame to frame admiring the artwork, large pictures of human embryos right after conception when cells grow into more cells to make life. Gold metal labels read, "Day Two" with one cell mirroring the other, then two cells that split. Others read, "Day Three" and "Day Four" and so on. I was captivated and wanted to be a part of this world.

I turned around when I heard a voice behind me. "Welcome, my name is Lauren, and you are?" She had electric blue eyes and black shiny hair that shimmered when she moved. She hesitated, and then reached out her hand to shake hands with me. I felt her sizing me up, and I knew my age was an indicator of why she hesitated. I could tell from her eyes that she might have wondered why I was there.

"Susan Ring. I made an appointment to learn about egg donation and I think I was supposed to go with the group, but I felt out of place," I said, thinking *why didn't I just say surrogacy?*

I got a hint fairly quickly, and this one became more evident by the second. The more I looked around, the more motherly I felt. I wished at that moment I had asked more questions over the phone instead of coming into the office.

"My partner, Tracey, and I own the center and I'm also a registered nurse."

"I see," I said. She led me to her office and offered me a seat. I admired the thank you letters and photos on the walls. Photos of happy families, babies, and toddlers like the ones you see in an OB/GYN office. Seeing them made a difference for me. What a wonderful thing to do for another couple. What a cool job she had, I thought, and to own the business, too. Wow. I would love to do something like this one day, I thought. I wondered what her life might be like.

She began the interview after I filled out a short questionnaire with my name, address, and phone number, but we got to the important question right away.

"Your age, Susan?"

"Thirty-eight."

She looked up at me with despairing eyes. "Oh, I'm so sorry, but our cutoff for donating eggs is twenty-eight, and we typically like the donors to be in their early twenties. It's pretty standard everywhere." She lifted her dark, perfectly shaped eyebrows while she fiddled with her Prada sunglasses. She probably had somewhere to go and wanted to get this meeting over with. Somehow I must have slipped through the cracks. I thought.

"Um, yes, I thought that the women in the other room were much younger than I am." I didn't know what else to say. It seemed like everything I said was stupid.

She smiled, not saying anything back to me. I now thought being there was a silly thought on my part, and I felt a flush of embarrassment imagining my eggs were probably as viable as dinosaur eggs. I seriously thought, *since when was I too old for anything?* There was and odd silence between us. I sensed she was in a hurry. It was the kind of silence that says, 'it's time to go.' I slowly grabbed my things to leave, and she stood up.

As Lauren and I left her office, I saw another woman in the hallway and I moved over to the side to let her pass. I heard Lauren from behind me say, "Tracey, this is Susan Ring, she's interested in egg donation. Susan, this is Tracey, my partner." I kept thinking, why didn't I just say surrogacy?

She barely touched my hand and smiled a tight, toothless, pink lipstick smile. "Hello," I said.

When she nodded back, the aroma of Angel perfume came in strong. I looked at her again closely because she resembled Jennifer Aniston. She looked busy and focused on whatever she was working on and obviously needed Lauren's help on something that probably involved much younger eggs.

I wondered if they each had kids and wondered what kind of life Tracey had. Lauren appeared to be around my age, and Tracey maybe a few years younger. Both of them were dressed impeccably and looked like dark and light version of twins. Both had on tight black pants and leather-spiked boots, the really feminine kind. Both had on ribbed turtleneck sweaters, one in beige the other in black looking like something out of a fashion magazine.

"Well, thank you so much ladies, but it looks like I might be ten or more years too late to donate my eggs. Thank you for your time." They both hesitated until Lauren broke the silence when she said, "So very nice to meet you, Susan."

I left their office wondering how it might be to have everything I wanted. They sure seemed to have it together, but because I never knew what it was like to have everything I wanted, I wasn't missing anything. I felt like I only knew how to survive.

I went there to look into surrogacy but never brought it up because they didn't mention that their agency represented surrogacy, and I didn't ask. I should have said something about it but I felt like I didn't fit in there. I considered calling them the following day, but I doubted I would follow through out of total embarrassment.

About a week later, after dropping the boys off at school, the phone rang. It was Lauren. I wondered why she would be calling me.

"I called to talk to you about surrogacy, not egg donation," she said.

My ears went into full listening mode. "Really, you do surrogacy also?"

"Well, no, but we want to add surrogacy to our services and we thought you'd be a fantastic choice for a surrogate mother. You have kids, right?"

"Two, yes!" I said, excited. "Surrogacy has been in the back of my mind since I had my first son, but I don't know much about it. How funny you should bring it up." It felt like I had to be aloof, not so excited and quickly followed up with, "That sounds like an interesting offer, Lauren, I'd like to learn more about it."

"I'd be happy to get educational information for you. We've done egg donation for years and have had many requests for gestational surrogates. In fact, we already have a waiting list. If you accept, you'll be our first surrogate mother. There are a lot of women who need help with egg donation and/or carrying a child to term to complete their family."

"I thought maybe the two go hand in hand, egg donation and surrogacy," I said.

"They do. When you came to the office to visit, we knew that you would be the perfect candidate for surrogacy. One of the requirements is you have to be medically cleared by a reproductive endocrinologist who specializes in infertility. Oh, and you would have to pass a psychological exam, and have a discussion with a therapist. After that are contracts and meetings with attorneys."

"Sure, I understand." I wondered what it was they looked for to clear a woman for surrogacy. I had an excellent pregnancy history and no complications with my boys. "I'd like to talk to someone who has gone through being a surrogate mother, if that's possible?"

"Of course. We're happy you might consider it."

"It's something I've been wanting to do."

"I'll look into getting someone to talk to you," Lauren said.

I was excited. Surrogacy found me again, and it felt like I was moving forward with my life, doing the things I wanted to do. I knew surrogates received compensation for their efforts, but I had no idea what it was, and still wanted to do it. Anything would help, and I could start putting money away for the boys' college funds. Seemed like a win-win to me.

7

Surrogacy Education

I didn't know a lot about surrogacy, but knew I could do it as long as it was gestational surrogacy. There wasn't a lot of information available online at the time, so I read all the books I could find on the subject. I thought it was a good idea to talk to someone who had actually been through the process. After I talked with the surrogate Lauren put me in touch with, Amy, I decided that surrogacy would definitely be for me. I asked Amy the typical questions people might ask like, "Why did you want to do this?" She answered, "I wanted to help a couple in need."

There wasn't anything profound about her replies except that she mentioned she felt called to do surrogacy only one time. She found it time-consuming and said, "It took too much time away from my family. It's a 24/7 job once you are pregnant." I didn't know exactly what that entailed, but I knew I would be pregnant for a certain amount of time, and I was willing to commit that time to being pregnant. I also asked her how she felt after the birth. "How was it, letting go of the baby?" I asked.

"It was easy because I knew this wasn't my child from the start," she said. That was how I felt too.

I started the medical clearance procedures and I found the

reality of it and the process of becoming a surrogate mother was more complex than I originally thought. This was only the start. There were many medical hoops to jump through and a checklist of tests to be cleared for to have my uterus found healthy. Some tests were invasive, such as the dye test of my uterus to check its overall health; I had to drink a lot of liquid to fill my bladder, and then dye was injected to see how everything flowed from the tubes to the uterus. There was one main blood test for infectious and autoimmune diseases. After I cleared the medical hurdle, I was set up to find a match with intended parents who needed a surrogate. Years later, knowing what I know about the match process, I can't stress enough how important this step is to find like-minded people work with. The match is *the* most important part of the process.

Making a Match

Lauren and Tracey received a procedural checklist from another agency on how to conduct a surrogacy match. It involved me meeting with three couples in one evening and spending an hour with each one to get to know them. Sometimes a surrogate might have a strong connection with one couple over another or more in common with one than another. Lauren and Tracey set up the meetings and instructed me before I met the couples that I was to choose one couple after I talked to all three.

I thought right away, *How can I do that?* Was one couple more needy or deserving than the other? They all needed a surrogate mother to help them have a child/family. Was I looking for a glowing connection, like finding a good friend in an hour?

After I met with all three couples, I wanted to work with the last couple I chatted with. However, it turned out they didn't have the funds for the journey, so they were eliminated through the agency.

I chose the second couple I met, but they decided they

wanted to save money by working without the agency. During our initial interview, I told them that I lived across the street from an elementary school and ran my daycare in the town I lived in. They asked which town, and I told them not thinking much of it. After our meeting together, I found out they called all five elementary schools in my town and found me through the receptionist at the school by requesting my daycare so they could get in contact with me without the agency.

I couldn't blame them, surrogacy is not cheap, but I still didn't know much about the process. I figured if they tried to cut out the agency, they might also do it to me down the line. My first instinct was to stay with the agency because I thought it was safer. I told Lauren and Tracey what happened. I knew it was their job to make sure things went smoothly and keep all parties working together so things were fair and safely done. There were so many details that I knew nothing about and this incident made me feel uneasy, so that couple was out. Lauren and Tracey dropped them from their list.

Michael and Jackie were the last couple from those first meetings. I told the agency I did not connect well with them because something felt off about them.

Tracey urged me to meet with them one more time to see if we might have more in common, so I agreed and we met a second time.

Jackie appeared casual, professional, and reserved at our second meeting. It was awkward. Petite and articulate, she folded her hands in her lap like my mother told me to do, though I never did. I focused on her perfect, straight, black, chin-length hair and wondered about her age. Wrinkles showed around her mouth heavily when she frowned. She often interrupted her husband with comments like, "I don't think that was the way it actually happened, Michael, *honey*." She put great emphasis on the word "honey." Michael would stop speaking, look at her for a strange silent long pause, and then continue to speak.

He was the talker. He reminded me of a big teddy bear

because he had to be at least 6'3" with a large frame, thick eyebrows, and dark hair and eyes. He was warm and engaging. As our interview progressed, I felt him drift away when I was talking. His eyes held a faraway gaze like he was daydreaming. Yet when he talked, he was excited about what he said.

I thought about meeting new couples, but Tracey assured me that Michael and Jackie would be a great couple to work with, and they were ready to do the match. Michael was a successful entrepreneur. Jackie worked for a small pain management practice as a specialty therapy nurse. He grew up in Beverly Hills and his family still lived there. She grew up in Boston and moved to Los Angeles several years ago. They lived in a downtown condo and had been married for three years. This was all I knew about them.

I still didn't feel a connection, but the agency urged me to think about working with them. I figured they knew more about forming a partnership through surrogacy than I did, so I went with the agreement to work with them.

Support System

It is important to have a support system in place for the surrogacy process. Although Lauren and Tracey were available to help because they lived so close, I also had to make sure things were going to work at home.

My mother was my biggest supporter for surrogacy, though not right away. When I first told her I was going to be a surrogate mother, she put her hands on her hips and looked at me like I'd lost my mind. Then she pointed at me like so many times before and shook her finger saying, "Susan Ann, you are not going to give up my grandchildren."

"Mom, they wouldn't be your grandchildren," I said as I sighed, and resisted the urge to roll my eyes. Chances were if she saw me do one good roll of the eyes she'd get mad and not listen to me.

"Well, any baby you give birth to you should keep. Surrogacy is just wrong and it's not normal. You would never be able to give the baby up after it is born," she said firmly with confidence that she was right. "You are way too much like me."

Obviously, she didn't know me very well. I wasn't just like her. She'd told me many times she'd never give a baby away if she carried it. I knew I would and could. That was the extent of our conversation until I explained to her how it was done. It was like that with surrogacy. It seemed I had to take the hand of the person doubting me, even my own mother, and explain with detail or pictures how surrogacy works. She came around after my first surrogacy after she saw the miracle in helping someone else have a child.

A few weeks later, it was time to talk to Terrie about my plans of becoming a surrogate mother. I waited to tell her because I wanted to make sure it was something that was actually going to happen. It was early spring and it looked like I was going to be approved, but I was only half way through the pre-matching process. I knew surrogacy would have to be a group effort. I waited until the boys went to sleep so I could talk to her alone.

We were sitting on the couch in the living room, relaxing after a long day.

"So, remember I told you a few months ago about wanting to be a surrogate mother? Well, I found a place that I will be working with."

Terrie looked at me slightly shocked.

"What? You are really going to go through with it? I can't believe you would do something like this, Susan." She looked at me even more surprised. "You'll never be able to give up the baby. You're way too motherly."

Her look of shock and surprise turned disapproving, and I felt my walls go up. I didn't understand her response because as my best friend I thought she knew me. This wasn't your everyday conversation, but I also didn't talk to her a lot about it. It was something personal that I kept deep inside. I knew surrogacy was a last stop option for someone to have a biological family. Being able to help a family bring their biological child into the world was important to me.

"Yes, I will, Terrie. I thought you knew me better than that. I would never try to do this if I didn't think I could. I've thought about it for years. It's the kind of thing that is an ultimate gift for someone else who needs help. It isn't just something out of the blue."

She crossed her arms and I could tell she was tuning me out.

"I hope you understand this is something I really want to do. Maybe we can talk more about it later."

It took her a few days to get comfortable talking about it, but as she asked me questions, it seemed she was beginning to accept it. Her main concern was that I would definitely give up any baby I give birth to. She didn't have children, so I know it was hard for her to understand. It was important to me that those I loved who were closest to me would be okay with my decision. I needed a good support system. After she warmed up to the idea, I decided to talk with the boys.

The next evening while I was putting them down for bed before story time, it felt like a good time to talk to them.

"Guys, I have something important to talk to you about," I said. They both looked at me waiting. They knew it had to be important because I didn't talk to them like this unless it was.

"I want to be a surrogate mother for a couple who can't have children themselves." I took a breath and continued. "It would mean having a baby for someone else."

"Is it going to hurt mommy?" Brian asked. "Because I don't want you to hurt." His eyes were serious and innocent at nine years old. It struck an emotional chord with me that he understood this much. I was touched.

"Yes, it does hurt when I give birth, honey, but it only hurts for a short time, and then I forget all about most of it and a beautiful baby comes into the world. It would be like when I gave birth to you and Steven." He looked satisfied, but still had an unsettled look. I waited for more questions.

"But, Mommy, why do you want to hurt?" Steven asked.

"A woman can't have a baby without hurting a little bit." I was glad I consulted the psychologist beforehand with age-specific questions and answers. I could see they wanted to know more but maybe didn't know how to ask the questions.

I said, "When the people's baby is teeny tiny, the doctor puts it into my tummy to grow because the other woman's tummy doesn't work and mine does." I was using hand gestures to show them how it would work. "When the baby is born, Mommy hands it over to the real mommy and daddy. I just help them grow their baby."

"Oh. But no one had me except you, right, Mommy?" Steven asked.

"Right, honey, I gave birth to you and Brian. Mommy and Daddy made you and I grew you."

My boys meant the world to me, and I loved them fiercely. I wasn't going to do surrogacy unless they were okay with it. But they were still so little it was hard for them to understand. I needed to help them see how it might affect us as a family.

What I didn't realize until later was how much they truly did understand what was happening. Often people would direct questions to them during my pregnancies. I told them it was important to be honest with people when they asked questions. During my first journey when I was noticeably pregnant, people asked many questions and they were by well-intentioned people who wished us well. Most of them were astonished with the boys' truthful and straightforward answers. They understood it better than some adults.

"Wow, looks like your mom is pregnant again, bet you all hope it's a girl," onlookers often said.

"It's not ours. My mom is having a baby for a lady who can't grow her own baby. Her tummy is broken," Steven would answer loudly with his blond head bobbing alongside my pregnant belly. The boys took turns answering people. At first it was fun, but after a while they got tired of it because the onlookers had too many questions. The boys became child experts at surrogacy and infertility. I often heard them talking to their friends when they were over at our house. They knew the tiny embryo was put into Mommy by a doctor and became a baby over time. They were onboard as much as they could be.

We were ready to move ahead.

8

More Waiting

It took several more months to go through the steps with the agency—more medical clearance items, lab appointments, attorneys, psychologists, a background check, and more medical exams to make sure my womb was healthy and what I thought at some point, perfect.

I was prescribed bio-identical hormones in pill form and shots that I would take to get my uterus ready and plump for the embryo transfer along with meds to stop my ovulation so my egg didn't accidentally get into the mix.

Psychological Testing

I found myself sitting in Dr. Westin's office, the appointed psychologist, when I completed the Minnesota MultiPhasic Personality Inventory (MMPI). She sprang a ten-page questionnaire on top of that. I went through the pages and stopped when I hit page nine. I hesitated to answer some questions about childhood abuse because I wanted to appear the perfect candidate, and I didn't want to throw up a red flag and appear wounded. By this time, I'd put a lot of time into the process and didn't want to be turned down because of something I had no control over. The sexual abuse by my stepfather when I was a child affected me in ways I continued to feel for years. *Who would ever know if I didn't answer truthfully?* I thought. My pen danced over the top of the boxes wondering if I wanted to answer. I was trying to be honest with myself about the abuse, but it was a hard thing to talk about with those who didn't understand. I thought I was well over it, but the memories still seeped in and things I was working on were sometimes a great struggle. I'd gone to therapy trying to put myself together and it took years to be okay with myself.

I didn't go into detail on the questionnaire because remembering the abuse was painful, and did it really matter? Abuse is abuse. I hid it all those years thinking it was my fault because my abuser manipulated me into not telling, and to believe it was my fault. I'm sure I still probably had issues to work on about this subject.

I decided to check yes, admitting I was sexually abused. I anxiously waited to hear back from the psychologist thinking everything was probably done and over, and that I'd be turned down.

A few weeks later, I met Dr. Westin in her office to go over the results of the testing. She sat at her desk putting all the paperwork together and then turned her chair around to talk to me in her small, cozy office where everything was so clean and white—the loveseat I sat on, the pillows, her chair, the curtains, even the carpet. We talked about the test and she said I passed. She asked me if I had questions and finally brought up the abuse toward the end of our conversation.

"You know, Susan, admitting it is half the battle."

"Yeah, I guess so," I said with a nod and thought that was true. I was happy to finally admit it on paper and out loud. I looked at the desk behind her and saw the corner of the room full of pictures of her children and possibly grandchildren.

"Do you have concerns about it or do you need to talk further about it?" she asked.

"No, I'm fine. I've gone through therapy. Thank you."

"One more question for you," she said. "Susan, why exactly do you want to be a surrogate mother?" Her short white hair framed her forehead and she looked at me eye to eye.

I raised my eyebrows and moved my head back to think about how to answer her question.

"I really want to help someone have a baby and make a family. I want to leave some kind of a legacy, and I want to make my life matter to someone else, like it mattered to me when I gave birth to my own children. It gave me life when I became a mother, you know?"

She smiled like she knew and nodded.

"And, I just don't think I'm done being pregnant," I added.

"Okay, then, you've passed all the testing and it looks like I will approve that you move on to the next step to being a surrogate mother."

Legal Contracts

The legal portion of our surrogacy arrangement between me, and the intended parents, Michael and Jackie, was next. We had separate attorneys to avoid conflict of interest. All legal and contract expenses were paid for by the intended parents.

I met the attorney, Gregory Lazar, late one night with Lauren and Tracey at their office when the boys were with their dad. No one was sure whether he would be my attorney or Michael and Jackie's. Tall and handsome, he wore a brown pinstriped suit. We sat down at the conference table.

"So, are you legally divorced, Susan?" he asked.

"Technically no, but I'm separated and not living with my husband," I said. He looked concerned and pushed back in his chair. I hesitated, knowing that look especially after all of the work I'd gone through to get approved. This was the last step before we did an embryo transfer.

"I'm sorry," he said. "You can't go into any kind of contract in California without your husband's signature or approval."

California is a 50/50 state and a civil law contract needs to be signed to be a surrogate mother. The courts need to know whether a woman is married or living separately from her spouse. "You didn't legally separate, right?"

"No, we didn't." I sat back in my chair to think it over. We looked at each other and Lauren looked on. "He won't divorce me. It took me forever just to get child support, and I'm done paying a divorce attorney for nothing." I felt let down. The last part of the deal was going to fall through because of this?

"There is one thing you can do, Susan, but you will have to go back to court and ask for a divorce if that is what you want. Your husband won't have to agree. It's called bifurcation." The attorney stood and picked up all of the papers on the table and put them back into his briefcase.

Sometimes I thought I might give up on the journey because it was so time-consuming and turned out to be a lot more work than I thought and I was not compensated for my time up to this point. But I wasn't going to give up, I'd come this far and I wanted to get divorced anyway, so I made plans to go to the courthouse and file for a date.

It took months to get a court date and sure enough Robert's attorney changed our court date to delay it further and finally, the date came. I was given a divorce via bifurcation. It required me standing up in court before the judge stating it was what I wanted, to end our marriage. I knew as I was standing there before the judge by myself, that I was hurting Robert. I could see it in his face as he stood at the next table with his attorney. I felt the hurt as well, but I also saw it as a new beginning.

I was legally divorced in October 1999. I received the papers in the mail with the stamp of California's approval. There was something real and wonderful about making my divorce official. I felt good about moving ahead. I was able to sign the surrogacy contract as a single woman. Having a contract gave me a sense that everything was officially legal. That once the contract was signed no one would be able to change their minds about the things we signed off on and agreed upon. It helped me trust the process, as well as Michael and Jackie.

Eight months had passed from the first day I went to the agency. I didn't feel like there was any hurry, but I wasn't getting any younger.

Our first journey wouldn't start for another few months. Michael, Jackie, and I got to know each other a little bit more during that time. They took me and the boys out for dinner a few times but we never really bonded the way I hoped. Jackie would bring magazines and read the local paper to occupy her time looking for million dollar houses she wanted to live in while we talked. Every so often she'd turn to Michael and say, "How about this one? Does this look right for our new family?"

It wasn't what I expected, but I didn't encounter any major problems like some people experience with surrogacy. Lauren and Tracey told me there were so many things that could go wrong, like the intended mother having issues about another woman carrying her husband's baby. Along with control issues where a couple might want a surrogate to do things she isn't willing to do like not color her hair because of the chemicals or to eat vegan or cut out all junk foods. I knew myself well enough to speak out if I felt there was an issue and would address it head on. Jackie didn't seem to have any issues with any of the things that Lauren and Tracey talked about. I just let it be, knowing nothing was going to be perfect and if something came up we could just work it out as we went along.

9

Surrogacy Journey #1

The Beginning of Journey #1

I started the medications a few weeks before the transfer of embryos into my body, and followed the doctor protocols for bio-identical hormones. The needles bothered me because I'd never given myself a shot before. The hormones prescribed were being to be used with a 3-inch long, very thick needle. It seriously freaked me out. I asked the doctor if it was available in pill form. It was, but apparently the infertility doctor protocol calls for oil form via needles because it provides more favorable results. It required one needle to draw the oil out of the bottle, and then I had to transfer it to another needle to shoot it into the top of my buttocks/back hip every day for twelve weeks. After I prepared the needle, it took me about three hours before I summed up the courage to stick myself. I got better at it as time went along. After the numerous appointments and blood tests, along with checking the lining of my uterus, it was time for our first transfer of embryos. Michael and Jackie were not present for our first transfer with Dr. Cohen, a reproductive endocrinologist at the center. They had to work.

Embryo Transfer

The embryo transfer was to take place in the fertility office in a small exam room. It wasn't a surgical suite, but it didn't appear they needed one. Dr. Cohen was a handsome doctor at the prestigious, popular, and well-respected fertility clinic. He stood tall, about 6' with salt and pepper hair and a warm, inviting smile. I was attracted to him immediately, but I knew nothing could happen between us. I couldn't help but notice, though, that he wasn't wearing a wedding ring. One of the nurses must have seen the look on my face after I met him, because, she said to me, "He's married but doesn't wear his ring during medical procedures." She's seen this before, I thought.

I smiled and nodded trying to look like I didn't care. I wasn't having any luck with men anyway and my chances would be very limited once I became pregnant. I hadn't seen Adam for months and figured I was better off without him.

Tracey, from the agency, attended the transfer with me. She stood above my head where I couldn't see her while I was laying on the exam table.

Before Dr. Cohen began the transfer of embryos, he told me he would be transferring three human embryos (Michael's sperm and chosen donor egg) into the catheter and then into me. He told me one embryo was of questionable quality. Tracey was supposed to be there as support because Michael and Jackie couldn't make it due to work, but it seemed her attention was not on our transfer as Dr. Cohen inserted the flexible catheter into my body. I felt like the third man out: It seemed like Dr. Cohen and Tracey had some kind of communication thing going on between them. Something I was clearly not a part of. So, I ignored it.

At one point, Dr. Cohen's smile was huge. He wore a silly grin that got my attention immediately as he fished around between my legs. He was doing the transfer without an ultrasound, so he couldn't see what he was doing on a screen. It was at a time when ultrasound screens were being used on an as-needed basis. While his hands were moving to find the cavity of my uterus deep inside my body, he fumbled around trying to hold the catheter of embryos at the same time. I noticed he was looking straight up at Tracey and not me—longingly. I sensed he was not thinking about what he was doing, and I felt a pain deep inside. "Ouch," but automatically held back how much it really hurt. I turned back to look at Tracey behind me to see what he was staring at.

And there was the gorgeous Tracey, who had chestnut brown, silky, shoulder-length hair, pursing her full crimson lips in a kissing motion, tilting her head from side to side like she was kissing the air with closed eyes. Her hands were up, one in an O position and the other thrusting a finger into the O-shaped hand. I'm sure it was an inside joke. I took it as a "fucking" gesture regarding the exam and my open legs. She opened her eyes and saw me looking at her in surprise. She stopped immediately, but Dr. Cohen had already made the mistake.

He withdrew the catheter from inside my body and apologized profusely saying, "So sorry, Susan, I went through your cervix with the catheter instead of up and around where your uterus is."

With no pain meds, he stretched his hand and fingers back in as deep as he could inside my body to stitch up my cervix. It was painful and I was bleeding. I had my feet on the exam table, with my knees bent struggling to hold my butt up in the air as far as I could while Dr. Cohen stitched. It was very strange position to hold while wondering if he was doing it right.

After he stitched me up he said, "Typical transfers don't go like this, and you probably won't become pregnant." He looked down at the ground and added, "You should heal up fine in about ten to fourteen days, and we'll do this transfer again with the left over frozen embryos."

All I could think about was the possibility of human lives in cell form bouncing around somewhere in my body or worse, on the exam room floor.

Afterward, my pelvis and abdomen ached hard. It felt like a super heavy period with a lot of major cramping. As I was getting ready to leave, one nurse confided in me, "You won't be pregnant. It's almost impossible because the embryos didn't make it into your womb," she said.

I healed in ten days. And, went straight to the doctor's office with news: a positive pregnancy test. Out of three embryos, against all odds, one made it into my womb. We were pregnant with one baby.

Everyone in the clinic was surprised I was pregnant because most of them knew about the accident with the embryos, but they didn't know why it happened. I knew why.

I was glad he had told me there was a mistake, because I didn't know what to expect from my first transfer procedure. But I know what I saw that day—flirting at its worst. I decided to keep it to myself because I didn't know all the facts, and I didn't want to sound gossipy to an agency owned by two women. I justified it by thinking maybe it would have happened anyway, but he was definitely more tuned into her anatomy than mine. I wondered if they were having an affair.

As far as I knew, the clinic did not tell Michael and Jackie about the accident with the embryos, but I never asked. After Michael and Jackie learned I was pregnant, they went with me to almost every appointment to check on their baby, except the regular blood work appointments. By the time I was twelve weeks' pregnant, I was ready to transfer to my regular OBGYN, Dr. Harrison. The last time I was at his office, I told him about my plans to be a surrogate mother. I was his first surrogacy patient after having practiced for more than thirty years. Friendly and easy-going with thinning gray hair and glasses, he asked if we wanted to know the gender of the baby after he examined me.

Michael and Jackie said, "Yes," simultaneously while we were sitting in his office together.

"It's a boy," he said excitedly. I looked at Jackie. She had no immediate reaction of joy or sadness, but to me she looked disappointed. She looked down at the floor.

"Jackie grew up with girls and wanted a girl, but that's okay, honey, we'll have another," Michael replied when he saw Jackie didn't respond. He patted her back as he said it. She didn't move, just looked straight ahead.

Dr. Harrison and I looked at each other with the kind of look parents give each other when both understand that we don't choose the gender of our babies. We are happy to have any gender, grateful for a healthy baby. I felt a little let down, like I did something wrong. I knew I didn't do anything wrong, but I thought she was being ungrateful.

My pregnancy with their little boy was uneventful and everything went smoothly. I felt so good being pregnant again! It'd been almost eight years since the birth of my son, Steven.

Toward the end of the pregnancy, I started to want to be pregnant again before I even gave birth. The power of being pregnant and growing a human for another person was amazing, beyond words.

I thought about all the reasons why I wanted to be pregnant again so soon. Perhaps one reason I loved it so much was because my large belly kept me safe from being in a relationship with a man. Most men didn't give a pregnant woman a second look. Most people assume a pregnant woman is taken.

The other side of me missed being with a man, being loved in the way I wanted. Sometimes I'd schedule a full-body massage just to have another person touch me. When I felt particularly lonely, I called Adam. He loved seeing me pregnant and honestly didn't care that my body had changed so much. I was very sexual when I was pregnant due to all the hormones flowing through my body, another reason I loved being pregnant. I still had the most naïve belief that I'd find a man who would understand what I was doing, and would love that I was pregnant for someone else.

10

Evan's Birth

My water broke in Ralph's Grocery Store. The boys and I were shopping for Halloween candy. I stopped in aisle six and froze. Fluid started to gush all over the floor, thoroughly wetting my pants and the floor around me.

I was helping the boys with a game they were playing called, "Boo! Halloween Ding Dong Ditch." We cut out a white ghost from construction paper and called it Boo. Then we filled a baggie with goodies and ding dong ditched people we knew and included a Halloween note about keeping the game alive. We had played three times, when we stopped by the store to gather more goodies.

I knew what the start of labor felt like, that feeling of no return, and what the imminent birth of a baby felt like. This baby was coming. My tummy was round and hard, like a big beach ball stuffed under my big gray maternity shirt. Steven looked at me surprised and said, "Mommy, why'd you spill that water all over the grocery store floor?"

"No, honey, my water broke." I laughed softly as I explained what was happening to Brian and Steven. They looked at me puzzled. "The baby is ready to come," I said, wondering what my next move should be.

"You wet your pants, Mom," Brian said, clearly amused as he pointed at me. I think he was slightly embarrassed for me, too.

"My water broke before I had you and Steven too. It's water inside my tummy in a little sac where the baby lives, drinks, and swims during the pregnancy," I said. They stood looking at me in wonder.

An employee in the same aisle came over to see if she could help. "Is everything okay here?" she asked.

"Um, yes. I'm pregnant and my water just broke."

"Oh, my God! Let us call 911 for you." She took off running to the front of the store before I had a chance to tell her not to. I wasn't having contractions, so I walked up to the front of the store with the boys to tell them I wouldn't need an ambulance. "Can we buy this candy please?" I asked casually.

"Oh sure. Can we help you to your car?" the cashier asked.

"No thanks, I've got two great helpers and our house is just around the corner from here."

"Good luck, ma'am. Good luck boys!" A handful of people gathered to watch me waddle to the cash register as I sloshed in my shoes. They yelled out their well wishes, "Take care!" The boys got excited with everyone else because the baby was coming. I knew I had a few hours of labor to go before little Evan arrived. As we left the store I heard over the store's speaker, "Clean up on aisle six."

I called Lauren and Tracey when I got home. Tracey picked me up later that evening after contractions started. I got my bag packed and managed to put the boys to bed assuring them I would be fine, and let them know they could come see me the next day. Terrie would stay with them for the night, and Tracey would get them to school in the morning. We headed for the hospital in her jade-colored Jaguar; I had visions of getting her nice leather seats all wet.

I didn't have a birth plan, so when we got to the hospital, everything was in the moment, including having Michael and

Jackie in the room while I was in active labor. They put me into a regular birth room. I didn't mind too much that they were in the room because if I were in their place, I would want to see my baby being born too. The only awkward part was Michael constantly going to the end of the bed and looking intensely between my legs. I suspect he was looking for the baby's head but I was trying to focus on the birth. I was getting annoyed and it felt strange, and creepy with being in the way. It kept delaying the birth because it made me feel uneasy. I envisioned his head flying out the window into the street.

I almost asked him to leave, but Jackie said to him, "Um Michael, it'd probably be good for you to stay up here on this end of the bed until the baby is ready to come."

It's a good thing she said that because I didn't know what I was going to do if he didn't get out of my way.

I was in hard labor most of the night and a few times through the night they had to put a fetal monitor on his head and pull me to my left side due to the stress of labor. I gave birth to Evan the next morning. After ten hours of labor and one intensified short push, he came out.

Dr. Harrison put him on my belly in a panicked hurry, which surprised me because I didn't know what to expect once he was born. Tears of profound happiness came rolling down my cheeks just like they did when I had my own children. All of us stopped everything we were doing when we noticed Evan was in distress and purple. He wasn't crying right away like newborns usually do because the cord was wrapped around his neck. I had never seen a cord wrapped around a baby's neck. It was twisted, thick, and braided strong, wrapped around his little neck twice. Dr. Harrison made quick moves to free him, and then Michael snipped the cord. Evan's little purple body started to get oxygen and he let out a shriek, then a faint cry that grew stronger the more I held him to my skin and massaged him.

"Welcome, little one," I said with tear-stained cheeks. I

kissed him on the top of his wet, black hair and his cry got louder. He was born healthy weighing in at 8 pounds 4 ounces and 21 inches long.

I was in love with the miracle of birth, and I was hoping Michael and Jackie would be more overjoyed, but they seemed like they were simply happy. After Evan was freed from the cord, pink, and crying loudly, I looked at Jackie. She extended her arms out half way to hold her son. I handed him to her and watched her soften as she held him close in the crook of her arm with Michael looking on. She looked up at me after a few minutes and I smiled watching them bond with him.

I felt myself start to let go. I felt the space of time widen between us as he moved away from my womb, my body, and my arms.

Jackie looked at her new son and said to Michael, "Look, it's our son."

Our bonding time of nine months was over. Evan was with the boys and me for nighttime stories, endless baseball games and practices on cold, hard bleachers. He was there for lots of tummy hugs from the boys. I'd miss Boomer's doggie nose on the tip of my belly at night as I read in bed. He was much more protective when I was pregnant and slept close to me. Evan was with us for chores, errands, appointments, and massages for me to help me feel better during those times my legs ached while I carried him. He was always with me nestled deep inside, and I never felt alone. I told him little stories about him being so wanted, and I hoped the best for him and that I'd always remember his birthday and our pregnancy wherever he was in the world. I wanted him to know that while I grew, nurtured, and birthed him then handed him over to his parents, it was with the most genuine love and compassion.

Michael, Jackie, and Evan were now a family.

Late that afternoon at the hospital, I heard a gentle knock at the door. Half the day had passed since Evan's birth, and Michael and Jackie left to prepare the nursery at their home and left Evan in the nursery. The nurses brought him in every so often to be held and feed which didn't bother me a bit. I loved holding him and this way I could have personal time to talk to him. I decided not to breastfeed. I felt it was too bonding for me. They would be back the next morning to take Evan home after he had all his testing.

"Come in," I said.

It was Adam. I was surprised. I never told him I was going to the hospital, but he knew I was close to labor after I talked to him on the phone a few days before. He had contacts at the hospital and I'm sure he knew I'd end up in the hospital sooner or later. Pastors frequently visit the sick and dying, as well as new mothers. It seemed like he worked his on-again, off-again mistress into his busy schedule.

He always waited for me to call to initiate our affair, and as hard as I tried to let it die, I'd always end up calling him, and we'd fall right back into the old patterns of our affair.

"Hi," he said.

I smiled.

"Well, looks like you made someone's life brighter today."

I smiled again. "How did you know I was here?"

"Well, you know. I know people who know people."

"Right, I should have known that, especially at the hospital." I reached over to scoop up Evan out of his bassinet next to my bed. He was sleeping soundly. "Isn't he beautiful?"

"Yes, he is beautiful and so are you, Susan." He reached over and kissed me on top of my head. Evan yawned. I started thinking about how wonderful that moment might have been if I gave birth to his child, but knew the thought was crazy. I thought it was probably a good thing that he had a vasectomy after his second child.

"Birth is an amazing miracle," I said to Adam.

"Yes, it is," he agreed and put his hand lightly on Evan's newborn head as if to bless him.

"I love it so much. I feel so special, and it's so powerful." I thought of how I'd never been anything like that before—special and powerful.

"It's addictive, you know?" I said.

"No, I don't know, but you make it seem so easy."

"Having a baby is the one thing a man can't do that is more powerful than anything a man can do. Fascinating," I said gazing at Evan.

I often spoke to Adam like I was talking to myself, speaking out loud the real voice inside my head. I could say anything to him and he always understood.

"Yes." He smiled nervously and I could tell he was getting antsy.

He was always in a hurry and nervous when other people were around us, so he left as quickly as he came, but it was a special visit. It surprised me that he cared enough to stop and say hello.

Theresa brought the boys to see me later that evening and they were all able to meet Evan and welcome him into the world. Jackie was a bit worried about germs as any new mother would be, but I mentioned to her that it was important for the boys to have closure, too. They needed to see the baby who was with us for nine months. She didn't want to say yes, but finally agreed when I made sure the boys washed their hands. Steven was most amazed by the birth. "How'd that baby fit in your tummy, Mom?"

We left the hospital early the next morning. I was wheeled out in a wheelchair carrying Evan, per hospital protocol. When we got to the car, I handed Evan to Jackie. Michael and Jackie drove me home in silence except for Evan's baby coos and gurgles.

They dropped me off to an empty house. Theresa was at work and the boys at school. I cried the moment my key hit the lock and realized it was a lot harder than I thought to give up a baby after giving birth. I was able to do it, but I felt a strong loneliness. My hands weren't busy doing motherly things like taking care of the baby, on-demand feedings, bathing, and cleaning. My arms actually ached to hold him and love him like I did while he was growing in me. Being a surrogate ended more abruptly than I expected. It was then that I realized I was doing all in one short time what most parents have eighteen years to do in letting go of their baby. And it was completely normal, letting go. It's what I had prepared myself for as a surrogate mother.

My journey as a surrogate mother was done. It was time to go back to my regular life. Lauren left me a note about my after school daycare. She had taken care of the kids for a few hours while I was in the hospital with Evan. It was great to have good support and I could see why they say you need that before you start a surrogate journey.

I wondered if I might have a touch of postpartum depression, due to feeling so sad and lonely but I stayed on top of the feelings to try to figure it out. Being aware of it helped.

I'm a do-it-yourself kind of person, so I was convinced that my sad feelings were due to a huge drop in hormones after the pregnancy. I missed those pregnancy hormones, and it was always a letdown after birth, even with my own boys. I didn't notice it as much with them because I was busy, but after my surrogate baby, I felt different.

My mom must have heard it in my voice when I talked to her after getting home, so she flew into LA from northern California to visit for a few days. She wanted to see surrogacy for herself. She went with me for a short visit over to Michael and Jackie's to see the new family.

"This is beautiful, Susan. Seeing it makes a difference," she said.

It made me feel better that my mom finally understood. I think she really got it.

"Thanks, Mom. I loved bringing Evan into the world. I'm so glad you're here." I gave her a warm hug and was so happy she came to visit.

"Someone told me surrogacy is like having a bun in the oven, you know like the baby is a bun, and you are the oven," she said.

"No, Mom, that's just a cutesy thing to say. I didn't just bake a baby. Surrogacy is nothing like that. I grew a real live human being."

When she left to go back home, every day felt like the next, and my body felt dry from the inside out. I couldn't shake the stuffiness inside my head, like a fog-ridden dreary night. I called my doctor and he said, "Give it a bit more time, Susan." So I did, and time did help.

A few weeks later, I started to get back to everyday life. My doctor gave me a pill to dry up my milk, which helped a lot. One day rolled into the next and I started feeling better. I slipped back into my after school daycare and started making plans for the holidays. I couldn't help but think about being a surrogate mother again because I felt so good being pregnant. I wanted to be that way all of the time.

PART TWO

11

Surrogacy Journey #2

Michael and Jackie asked me to carry for them again a few weeks after Evan was born. I hesitated to say yes because I was still sorting out how I felt. Something told me to move on to another couple and to give it all more time. My emotions were running high, and I was still trying to sort them all out. I thought about it for a few weeks and ultimately figured it would be easier to say yes to Michael and Jackie because we'd already gone through one surrogacy and all of the pre-work would be easy to do. Once the doctor gave his approval for my health and to start another pregnancy, we reworked the contract and we were ready to go.

I didn't listen to my intuition, but I started my next journey anyway when Evan was six months old.

The Beginning of Journey #2

I was back in the infertility office accompanied by Michael and Jackie this time for our next transfer. This transfer was to be done by the center's owner, Dr. Edelman. The clinic office had been remodeled since the last time I'd been there. There were new walls, paint, sculptured glass, and new furniture along with a brand new surgical center. The nurse called me back and showed me to the changing room. After I changed my clothes into a gown, I carried my bag of clothes back into the room and put them to the side; the nurse moved them back into the changing room. She then motioned me to the large chair in the center of the room and I waited for what felt like at least an hour. I sat in the transfer chair made of soft, rich Italian leather. It was comfy. The room was clean like a surgical room should be and was accented by a warm overall beige color. The nurses didn't talk to me much with Dr. Edelman; he was pretty straightforward and was known for his lack of personality. His bedside manner was not the best, but he was supposed to be the best in the business per the agency.

Dr. Edelman's voice was deep and firm for a petite, thin-set man. "I recommend we put two embryos into the womb of your surrogate," he said to Michael and Jackie. He brushed his soft gray hair back with his fingers and then placed his hands firmly onto his hips.

Jackie flashed her usual disapproving look and said, "But we did three last time with the same surrogate and we only got one baby." It occurred to me at that moment that I had never seen her fully smile, except when their child was born.

"I didn't do that transfer, another doctor in our practice did," Dr. Edelman said. "And it's beside the point. That was then, and this is now."

"We want twins, doctor," Michael said.

"That's why you should transfer two. If you transfer three, you will get three," Dr. Edelman said with total confidence, like he knew they would stick to my womb if he put them all in. No one, not even the best doctor in the world, was supposed to be so certain about the success of an embryo transfer. Supposedly, no one could tell if any would "take" in a transfer. Putting embryos into a womb was like a craps game. Every time you roll the dice, you never know what you will get. Sometimes one embryo can split into identical twins, too, which happens quite often with in vitro fertilization (IVF). But Dr. Edelman was certain that if he transferred three embryos, we would have triplets.

The nurse started to prep me for the transfer and shifted my chair at an angle with my head tipped low down to the floor. It was really uncomfortable. I watched the doctor, Michael, and Jackie move to the back corner of the surgical room where they talked with their hands in what looked like a heated exchange. I figured Dr. Edelman would prevail because most people listen to their doctors, especially fertility doctors when it comes to transferring embryos. Furthermore, I had agreed in my contract to carry two embryos, not three. I couldn't hear what they were saying, but I was sure it was about how many embryos to transfer. This was something difficult to plan ahead because the embryos changed in quality every hour before transfer. The nurse had given me Valium to relax, which was the typical protocol for the procedure. It was like an invasive pap smear at the OB-GYN's office. The Valium was working, leaving me with no worries in the world. The calmness of the drug was so nice, and I wished I could just turn it on and off whenever I wanted.

I started to get dizzy. I lifted up my head and glanced over at the embryos in the small petri dishes inside the baby incubator next to my chair. An hour earlier, the embryologist let me look at the embryos through the microscope. I was fascinated, beyond excited, and drawn in as I witnessed the beginning of life at just three days old. The embryos were such small, amazing human cells. "Maybe babies," I called them, shaped in a perfect sphere like the earth, the sun, or a full moon. They divided into more cells right before my eyes under the microscope. Any leftover embryos would be put in cryo-storage for another time. I loved seeing new life and couldn't wait to be pregnant again.

I still wondered if I was doing the right thing by working with Jackie and Michael again. I kept wondering if Jackie was a good mother to Evan, a child not related to her because they'd used an egg donor. She seemed happy enough with him, but not the overjoyed kind of happy I hoped for. I felt like I was being a bit judgmental, but something wasn't right about her and I couldn't pinpoint it. Maybe it was because she didn't get the girl she was hoping for.

They used the same egg donor and Michael's sperm to create the embryos like they did with Evan. They would be full biological siblings. Jackie mentioned to me that she tried to get an anonymous donor that looked as close to her as possible. I saw a few pictures of the donor, and she didn't look anything like Jackie except for the same dark hair. The egg donor was young and beautiful in her cheerleading uniform. The other picture looked like a prom picture from high school. I wondered if they did anything to choose the gender of the embryos this time, but I didn't ask.

I looked over at the three of them still in the corner of the room and saw a nurse bring something for them to sign. More paperwork. Surrogacy was full of consents and authorizations. Michael and Jackie signed and handed the paperwork back to the nurse.

Dr. Edelman came over and put my chair at an angle with my legs straight up toward the ceiling and my head down close to the floor. The blood rushed to my head while he prepared the final items for the transfer procedure. It was so awkward hanging up in the air like that but I was glad they figured out the issues so we could move forward.

Everyone stayed so quiet as the embryologist opened the incubator and slowly siphoned the embryos into the catheter. The situation made me feel like I had to hold my breath because this time it was much more professional. She handed the catheter containing the embryos to Dr. Edelman. His eyes stayed fixed on the catheter while the nurse stood by him. He glanced at the other nurse, who moved out of his way without a word, and then moved between my open legs stretched up to the ceiling. Michael and Jackie stayed near the door away from me. A nurse squeezed a hard pillow shape between my thighs to keep them open and in place, which was incredibly uncomfortable. The blood rushing to my head made me feel delirious. I tried to see the monitor but I could only glimpse at a corner of the screen. The nurse said, "Ready, doctor."

"The embryos are in the catheter and ready to be inserted into the womb," Dr. Edelman said with a serious face. This transfer was different than the first one because an ultrasound-guided machine let the doctor view the embryos during transfer. All I could see on the black and white screen was the outline of my womb and a little straw shape inside, which must have been the catheter swishing around.

"Completed, all three are in," Dr. Edelman said after a few minutes of silence. He handed the catheter to the embryologist to inspect for remaining embryos, snapped off his gloves, and walked out of the room without another word. Michael and Jackie followed.

"Three?" I said loudly, shocked. I looked up at the nurse. I knew Dr. Edelman heard me before he walked out the door.

"Yes," she said with her eyes wide and her eyebrows raised. "Your intended parents insisted on three, instead of the two Dr. Edelman recommended. They signed a medical waiver saying they understood it was against his medical advice."

I felt impending doom at the high possibility of carrying triplets and wondered why no one consulted with me. My heart beat hard. Shocked, I didn't know what to say. I thought the doctor had the last say with how many, not Michael and Jackie. It wasn't like they could go in and pull one out now.

I was instructed by the nurse to stay in the chair for forty-five minutes and try not to move. I still felt woozy from the Valium and lying with my legs up in the air didn't help. I asked the nurse to move me because I was so uncomfortable.

All the hormones were going to my head. They were supposed to prepare my womb for pregnancy and help sustain it by puffing up the lining in my uterus to help facilitate a perfect home for the embryos. My lining number before the procedure, a fourteen, was too perfect. I had a feeling all three embryos had found a home for the next nine months. I already felt pregnant. That full feeling you get when you know something is alive inside your body.

The nurse moved me to my stomach. My head was down with my pelvis tipped up. I felt like a human vial being moved every which way. I still felt loopy then the blood in my body shifted and I felt better. The nurse and embryologist left the room, leaving me alone. It was so quiet with just the humming of the machines. I felt tired, deserted, and then fell asleep to the thought of carrying three babies.

12

Discovery

I was livid they transferred three embryos and yet I couldn't do anything about it unless I decided to bring legal action. I went straight to the agency and both Lauren and Tracey said there was nothing they could do. We could not reverse the procedure. I'm sure that Michael and Jackie just referred back to the last transfer, what worked then. They wanted twins, so they pushed three embryos, but they didn't know the whole story of the first transfer and it wasn't my place to tell them. I decided to wait it out and see what happens at our next appointment.

Some weeks later, it was time to see how many embryos stuck to the lining in my womb. It was three days before Mother's Day in 2001. I was sitting in the lobby of the doctor's office waiting for Michael and Jackie. The doctor's office ran a blood test a few days ago to confirm I was definitely pregnant, but no one would know how many babies there were until we had medical confirmation with the ultrasound. I knew there were multiples by the way my body was reacting and because I was already bulging out of my regular clothes. I wondered what Michael and Jackie might think once we found out how many fetuses I was carrying. I was somewhat certain they'd be excited with multiples because they always talked about having a big family.

"Hurry up and wait" is a common saying in surrogacy that many, if not all surrogates experience. It's always waiting for something and wanting it to hurry up, like waiting for a good match with intended parents, contracts to be done, medical appointments, stopping the needles and medications, the transfer of human embryos, a positive pregnancy test, or waiting for the pregnancy to hurry up and be over, then maybe starting a new journey all over again.

I took in a long, deep breath and looked up at the clock on the wall in the clinic reception area where the transfer was done. It was 11:15 a.m. They were a little over an hour late. A woman who sat with me in the waiting room had already gone in and out of her appointment, making me wonder if I got the time wrong. The front desk told me to wait for Michael and Jackie, so I must have had the time right.

I sat alone watching the lighter-than-usual office traffic. The wooden chairs were set up in a U-shape around the outer wall of the clean, spacious white and beige contemporary office. Usually the office was packed with people who all stared at one another wondering what the other was there for. It was one of those unsaid things you do when your mind tries to figure things out. There is never anyone to confirm if you are right or not, but the set-up of the room encouraged everyone to look and sometimes stare at each other. Sometimes I'd be staring without even realizing I was doing it. I had to admit, it helped pass the time waiting, but I wished I'd brought a book. I started to feel irritated at the wait because my stomach was growling.

A middle-aged, extraordinarily tall couple walked in. She looked extremely serious, and the man following closely behind was holding a brown paper bag. I looked up and smiled, knowing it was probably a sample taken from him that morning. A nurse across the desk noticed him with his little brown bag and said, "Oh, good morning, Mr. Hutchens. Okay, we'll take that sample and notify you both of the results as soon as possible." He didn't say anything. He handed her the bag and then found a chair on the other side of the room. The woman started talking finances with someone at the front desk. In the fertility business, someone is always talking about finances. It was expensive to get pregnant artificially and even more so to get help to have a baby.

I sighed again, wondering where Michael and Jackie were. They were rarely late. If they knew they were going to be late, I was sure they would have let me know, especially at this first ultrasound appointment.

I went to the glass door of the lobby and tried to look over at the parking lot across the street to see if I could see Michael and Jackie's car. Nothing. I put my face up to the warm energy of the sun and closed my eyes taking in a long, deep breath, feeling the glow of the pregnancy through my skin. The feeling of being pregnant with multiples seemed to overfill an emptiness somewhere deep inside me. I felt warm and content, except that I was still hungry and was starting to feel starved beyond belief. I looked to see if there was candy at the front desk. None, dammit. I had already consumed a full breakfast and a few pieces of fruit. Spinach pizza sounded so good, and I laughed because I'd never eaten spinach pizza in my life. My cravings were intense and hunger constant. I felt different, like my body was drunk with life-sustaining hormones surging through my veins and bubbling up with happiness and joy that I'd never experienced before. I sat back down and waited.

I looked up at the clock again. 11:55 a.m. I made the decision to leave because I was starving and wanted to eat. I thought maybe they weren't going to show up. Just as I was working up the courage to leave, the nurse called my name and led me into the ultrasound room.

I was happy to finally get confirmation of what I already knew, but I wasn't sure I was ready for, and almost didn't want to believe was true. I kept wondering what the doctor would say, and what Michael and Jackie might say if there were triplets. I thought I'd be able to get Michael and Jackie to agree to me carrying all three because they already said they wanted twins and a big family. I felt one more wouldn't probably matter because I didn't want to even think about reduction. More than two almost always meant reduction in the surrogacy and the multiples world.

I threw my black stretchy yoga pants onto the chair in the corner of the exam room and pushed my underwear underneath the worn fabric of my pants, leaving my pink shirt and black velour hoodie on. I knew the routine and grabbed the neatly folded blue wrap on the table designed to go over the bottom of my body and hopped up on the table wondering if Michael and Jackie had shown up.

The nurse knocked on my door and propped it open. "They're here. Are you ready?"

"Yeah, I'm good," I said, annoyed at them for making me wait so long.

She opened the door just enough for Michael and Jackie to walk in. I had to admit it felt strange to be half-naked and knowing that soon I would have what looks like a seven-inch dildo with a condom on top and cold gel inserted into my vagina with them in the room. The seven-inch ultrasound wand is what some of my surrogate friends and I called "the weenie wand," a vaginal ultrasound that transmits a clear picture of the uterus to a monitor.

Since we'd already gone through a birth together with Evan, I lost some of my timid feelings because Michael and Jackie had been between my legs viewing the birth of their son. I made many of my decisions about surrogacy wondering how I would feel if I were in their position. The strange awkwardness of being a surrogate mother is that you give up a certain amount of privacy. Today, Michael and Jackie looked different and they were unusually quiet. They both only slightly smiled at me when they came into the room and when I said hello, neither one said hello back. I wondered if they had gotten enough sleep last night due to having a baby in the house. I felt uneasy.

We waited in silence until I broke it. "So, do you guys think twins or triplets?" I knew they wanted at least twins and I hoped for a response.

At that moment the doctor came in, and they didn't answer. "Hello, my name is Dr. Wiseman," he said.

No one answered, we just tipped our heads forward to say hello.

"So let's see what we have in here, shall we?" He looked at me. I hadn't seen him before. He was older, probably over sixty or so with silver-gray hair, a round face, and large black glasses. Although he seemed to have a jolly disposition, I still felt nervous.

He lifted the drape a little and inserted the wand into my vagina. My legs were spread in a position I had grown comfortable with. I felt the cold gel dripping down over the tip of the wand and thought about how I would end up wiping it from between my legs all day due to the generous amount he put on it.

"The numbers on your beta pregnancy blood test came back extremely high, so you probably have more than one," Dr. Wiseman said as he swished the wand around and looked at the screen. The position I was in felt uncomfortable, so I pushed myself up on the exam table, the paper crinkling with every move. Michael and Jackie stood next to the exam table in front of the monitor while the nurse kept watch by the closed door.

"Yeah, I'm sure all three took because I can feel the extra hormones in my body. It's a feeling I have," I said.

"Let's see for sure." Dr. Wiseman sounded relieved that someone spoke to him. The wand moved slowly to my left as we all peered at the ultrasound screen at what resembled a white circular mass that grew larger as he moved the wand toward it. I saw what looked like a solar system with a semi-black hole in the center possibly depicting a life with amniotic fluid and the fetus attached to a tiny umbilical cord connecting deep inside me.

The white matter looked like stardust swirling around the black dot in the middle, cocooning it and keeping it safe.

This was the moment I felt safest and at home.

He hovered around the black circular hold, turned the knobs, and steered the wand to what he saw as potential life, what he'd been trained to see.

"Okay here it is…one, A. See the heart beating?" He looked up at all three of us. I nodded, excited at the possibility of the fragile pulse of life, a very early fetal heartbeat at six and a half weeks. I marveled at how life knew to grow and replicate to become a baby and eventually live outside the womb. I always felt humbled at the miracle of life.

I looked over at Michael and Jackie, who were stone-faced, and then turned back to the monitor. A warm, troublesome feeling washed over me and I could hear my own heartbeat.

After the doctor measured the first sac, he moved the wand around and a few seconds later said, "Here is number two, B." The little heart was beating fast.

The image of the second sac burned into my memory. It was in the middle.

I saw Michael and Jackie look at each other in my peripheral vision. No one spoke. The doctor measured the second fetus without turning around and made notes in my file.

Did someone know something I didn't? Why wasn't anyone excited?

Dr. Wiseman swung around on his stool so we could all see the monitor and said, "And here is number three, C." He measured it from one end to the other and pushed a button so we could see a wider picture of all three nestled up in my uterus.

My heart skipped a beat and pounded in my ears.

I knew it. *Triplets.*

Still shocked with the confirmation, somehow I tuned him out as his words echoed with medical jargon they talk about when there are multiples. Then I heard him say, "C is up high on the uterine wall, and all three appear to be measuring on time."

When he said "three," I looked at Jackie to see her reaction. Her dark eyes conveyed the incomprehensible to me as a mother. She was not happy, and I didn't know why. As far as I knew and hoped, they wanted all of them. I could see Michael waiting for a response from Jackie. Standing there, they appeared to be two people I didn't know, not the two people I had a baby for less than a year ago.

Dr. Wiseman did more measurements and then printed the ultrasound pictures. As the pictures printed, he handed them to Jackie like he must have done hundreds of times for expectant mothers, but this mother looked different.

She looked and acted angry.

Why weren't they happy about this pregnancy? Jackie looked over at Michael like it was his problem, and he looked away at the wall. The silence felt so thick I couldn't breathe.

They all left the room so I could get dressed. I was happy to be rid of their negativity and breathe in peace, even if only for a few brief minutes.

After Jackie's reaction, I felt like the babies needed a mother, but pushed the motherly feeling away saying to myself, "Wake up, Susan, they aren't your babies."

What was I supposed to do and what the hell was going on? I pulled my pants up over my pregnant belly, unable to stop thinking about the worst possible thing that could happen. What if they didn't want any of the babies? "Come on, of course they do," I said out loud.

Michael and Jackie had waited a long time for a family and paid a lot of money to make these surrogacy journeys happen. Everything had been done with endless intention—the medical exams, cycling with the same egg donor, the countless meetings, the signing of the legal contracts, medical appointments, and everything else.

The most important thing was that the triplets were full siblings to their brother, and the triplets were biologically related to Michael. It made me feel a little more reassured. Of course they wanted their own children, but why were they acting this way?

Feeling hormonal, I felt like crying and I rarely cried. Instead, my head got hot, I started to sweat, and felt like I was going to pass out. I pulled off my hoodie and hung my head over my knees to catch my breath and looked at myself upside down in the mirror on the other side of the wall wondering how the hell I got myself into this.

I was happy all three were growing on time and appeared healthy, so I stood back up and tried to get myself together.

Breathe, Susan, breathe. I took a deep breath.

The thought of facing them all again in the exam room and the reality of carrying triplets suddenly hit me. Hard. Oh. My. God. My heart pounded hard, my breath quickened. I went back between my legs to breathe.

Calm, Susan. Calm.

After I calmed down some, I rested my hand on my tummy and pictured myself giving birth to triplets. Even with my initial excitement of three babies, my realistic side knew it was a super high risk to carry all three babies. I knew it'd be manageable with the parents on board.

I thought of Michael's and Jackie's desperation to have another baby. As I was making my decision about whether to move forward with them, Michael said, "Oh, did I tell you? We are going to hire a nanny if we have multiples."

That sealed the deal for me. That confirmed that they wanted a big family and needed a surrogate to help them, but any confidence I had about proceeding was riddled with holes of hesitation and I didn't know why. I wanted to be a surrogate again for someone, but I never should have taken a second journey with them.

My hopeful side kept saying there was no reason to think the second time wouldn't be just like the first, maybe even better. My desire to be pregnant again felt stronger than my own good judgment.

I knew it was better to listen to my intuition, but I dismissed it, convincing myself that everything would be fine. I was thinking about how easy it would be not have to interview with new couples. All of these thoughts kept going around and around in my mind and now it was too late to do anything about my doubts.

I heard a knock on the door and Michael and Jackie came back with Dr. Wiseman close behind. The exam room felt chilly again, and my warm sweaty head turned to cold as I sat directly underneath the air conditioning duct. I got goose bumps, so I grabbed my hoodie from the bottom of the exam table and pulled it on to warm up.

When I pushed my arm through the second sleeve, Jackie met my hand and jammed the ultrasound pictures into my open palm, saying through clenched teeth, "Here, you take them."

I froze, pretending I didn't hear what she said.

With my eyebrows raised, I stayed on the exam table motionless and holding the pictures up mid-air. Dr. Wiseman and I looked at each other puzzled. I looked back at Jackie, but she wouldn't meet my gaze.

"But these are...for you two," I said. "They are the only original copies." I offered them back to her but she turned away. All I could see was a frown and her jet-black, shoulder-length hair swishing away from me.

Holding their pictures made me feel like I did when I had my own boys' ultrasound pictures, but they weren't *mine*. Michael looked at me and said, "Just hold them, Susan. We'll get them back later."

I couldn't breathe. This was the woman who kept Evan's

ultrasound pictures on her refrigerator door under colorful baby magnets for everyone to see.

Dr. Wiseman broke the silence. "So, three babies, wow!"

Michael peered over at Jackie, who still looked angry, and muffled her reply under her breath. "Yeah, three, wow." She left the exam room. Michael glanced at us and then followed her. I wondered if they would wait for me, but I doubted it by their actions.

"Well, ahem…" Dr. Wiseman cleared his throat. "From what I just saw, I can only assume they don't want three babies."

"I don't know," I answered, still shocked and feeling screwed. "I do know they wanted twins, but I didn't know they transferred three until after they demanded it. They signed a medical waiver with Dr. Edelman saying they were aware, but why didn't anyone ask me?"

"I don't know, Susan. Doctors have different protocols even within one clinical practice and they have their own procedures of what they believe works best. It will always depend on the quantity and quality of every embryo, especially the quality, but there are never any guarantees. Dr. Edelman is the best," he said with confidence. "This is his practice and he is one of the most sought after experts in fertility."

"Oh, I don't doubt that. I am obviously very pregnant this time. But why didn't the doctor do what he felt was medically right for me as the surrogate mother?"

"Again, I can't say, but you can ask Dr. Edelman."

I figured the answer I'd get from Edelman wouldn't satisfy me and wondered what I should do next, so I decided to see what else Dr. Wiseman knew.

"Were Michael and Jackie told about the accident with the embryos during the first transfer with Evan over a year ago?" I boldly asked thinking they were never told and that was why they pushed for three to get two.

He grabbed my chart and started toward the door. "I can't

say because I wasn't there, but I did see a signed waiver saying the intended parents were warned that only two were recommended by Dr. Edelman. They pushed for more, then signed the medical waiver releasing liability knowing full well the huge risk of triplets."

He reached for the doorknob and stopped to look at me. "Dr. Edelman transferred three *after* the parents signed the waiver. He was very much against it."

"But why didn't Dr. Edelman ask me? It's my body and I never agreed per my contract to carry more than two. I left it to the doctor, not the intended parents." I squinted up at him in the harsh fluorescent lights.

"I suggest you talk to Dr. Edelman or your intended parents."

"But…"

Dr. Wiseman put his hand up. "Stop. Wait and listen for just a minute. Most importantly, right now you are pregnant with triplets. From a pure medical point of view a triplet pregnancy is not recommended." He turned around and opened the door, walking into the hallway with me following.

He turned and leaned in, looking at me eye to eye. He put one hand on my shoulder and shook his head. "The medical statistics of a triplet pregnancy do not support a good outcome for you or the babies, but let's wait and see what happens. We'll check you again in a few weeks." He turned away and walked me to the front desk. "In IVF, one, two or more can be lost naturally in the next four weeks or so. Be patient and we'll see you soon."

"Okay." I knew exactly what he meant with his medical authority and the grim statistic about triplets. I was also well aware that I would be challenged with a reduction from three to two fetuses. I couldn't wrap my mind around the possibility. I knew nothing about the procedure but knew the outcome was killing one fetus. I wasn't even sure Michael and Jackie wanted any of the babies now, so I hoped the loss would happen naturally.

I thought about my physical attributes. Tall at 5'10" with a long torso, I knew there was enough room to carry all of them. I turned around to see the doctor put a pen into his white lab coat pocket. He bowed his head toward me to say goodbye.

I didn't care what he thought. I felt giddy with all the extra hormones. I went to the lobby and as I suspected, Michael and Jackie did not wait for me. I pushed the glass door open and let it shut hard behind me. The sun hit my face and I glowed from head to toe. Engorged with hormones, I felt more maternal than ever, and starved! I tried not to think about the possibility of a reduction, but my mind sensed the looming danger and my mood changed. I looked around me twice as I stepped out into the parking lot, feeling and sensing danger everywhere around me. I opened the car door and searched through my purse and my car for food. Nothing. Shit.

I headed for the pizza parlor by our house.

I thought about how my body didn't know these weren't my babies. It just knew how to be pregnant. I felt a dark, sagging cloud above me, especially when I knew the doctors would be against me if I chose not to have the reduction. I didn't know who to talk to about this, and I had a good idea that Tracey and Lauren from the agency would side with the doctors. Everyone on the professional side would want the reduction. If it were my own pregnancy, I probably wouldn't have the reduction. After I got to the pizza place I remember eating the first piece of pizza so fast, I'm pretty sure I didn't even taste it.

When I got home, I checked my contract to see exactly what the wording was. It stated I would have to agree with any medical, written advice about abortion or I would be in breach of contract, but my only intention in agreeing with medical advice in the contract was about abortion, not reduction because of too many, and it was only if there were problems with me or the babies. There was nothing in the contract about selective reduction.

I became a surrogate mother to give life, not take it away.

13

My Body, Three Babies

The Friday before Father's Day in 2001 was my last appointment with the doctors at the IVF clinic before they let me move on to my own doctor for further care. I was twelve weeks pregnant with triplets. I dreaded the appointment because I knew Dr. Wiseman would bring up selective reduction, even though all the babies were healthy. I could feel them, and I knew they were thriving by the way I was eating and glowing.

Michael called and told me he would be at the appointment but Jackie would not.

While waiting for him to show up, I was called in for my appointment, so I went into the exam room alone. Dr. Wiseman walked into the room with great energy. "How are you feeling today, Susan?"

I felt nervous. "Good, just hungry all the time," I said with a limp laugh.

"Where are the parents?"

"Michael told me he was coming, but he isn't here yet, and Jackie couldn't make it."

Things were falling apart fast, and I wanted to state what was obvious, that things were not great and my immediate future looked shitty, but I decided against it. He sighed and grabbed the wand to measure each fetus.

A few minutes later, he sighed again and put down the wand. "They look beautiful and measuring right on time."

"Yes, they do look beautiful, don't they?" I sighed heavily wishing I were anywhere but there.

"You can stop your shots now and all medications."

"Well, there is some good news," I said happy that I had the go ahead to stop the twice daily shots. By this time, I felt totally numb from my buttocks to my ankle on the right side from the shots, so this news was particularly wonderful.

"We should probably talk about reduction now." He grabbed my chart from the table to make notations.

I looked down at the ground feeling my heart hit the bottom of my chest.

"Isn't it too late?" I looked up at his face. "I'm twelve weeks." I hoped I'd get the okay to keep things the way they were, that maybe something would change and I'd enlighten them all that it was too late.

"The specialists like to do reductions a little later, like between twelve and fourteen weeks. The outcome is better during this time. It's a common thing with IVF, Susan, when you get too many." It was an answer I didn't expect.

"Have your patients had this done?"

"Quite a few have gone through it, but most of them have been waiting a long time to be a mother and will do almost anything and take more chances with higher risk just to get pregnant. It doesn't usually happen with a surrogate mother because we typically transfer far fewer embryos. The outcome is usually better with a surrogate womb." He looked at me and I could tell he wasn't going to change his mind.

I didn't know what to say or do. I felt the urge to cry, suddenly hating everyone and everything around me.

I thought about when I asked to talk to another surrogate mother before I became one. She told me one surrogacy was enough for her. I should have taken that as a hint. She also mentioned that although her experience was good, it took too much from her body and her family to do it again. I wondered if there was something else she didn't tell me. I had a hunch there was.

"Susan, there is only one way to say this," Dr. Wiseman said, his forehead creased with concern. "It's my medical opinion for your health and that of the babies, a reduction is recommended."

He said this in the most caring and professional manner possible. I thought he might say this to me if I were his daughter. Then again, it probably would not have happened if I were his daughter.

"But they're all healthy," I said, feeling the corners of my mouth draw down.

"I know, but all we ever strive for in our practice is to have one healthy baby, no more than one, but reducing to two would be my recommendation."

How insanely ironic he was saying that to me when they worked with multiples all the time, and it was Dr. Edelman who put three into my body knowing they would take. I had more questions, but he advised me to talk to the specialist about reduction details.

I dressed slowly, thinking about how I was going to manage my life in the next few weeks. I wiped the extra gel from between my legs and balled up the paper drape so fast and hard that I nearly fell over. I threw it hard at the top of the round silver trashcan and it fell to the floor, rolling into a corner. When I turned from the trashcan, I caught a glimpse of myself in the mirror behind the door and saw the outline of my pregnant belly—a belly swollen with three babies. I took my hand and followed the outline of my belly in the mirror and studied the angry woman looking back at me. Her long hair over one eye and every line on her face intensified. How did I get here? What was happening?

I was willing to accept the fact that I created some of my own reality by saying yes to Michael and Jackie again, but some of this was done to me. Why was I always pushing the envelope, trying to do things beyond the ordinary? The armor of my pregnancy was helping me take up room in the world, but now all I wanted was to hide behind the bump. That same armor helped me feel fierce, but at the same time it seemed so large, ominous and unknown, making my situation scary.

"No" is a very difficult word to say when you've grown up as a people-pleaser.

I stepped back from the mirror and wondered what the hell I was going to do.

My thoughts were broken when I heard a crying baby from inside the office. I was surprised to hear it because I was told early on not to bring my children so it wouldn't upset women who are trying to get pregnant.

I opened the door to let myself out of the exam room and then opened the door to the lobby, where I saw Michael sitting with Evan in his arms. Evan cried uncontrollably and Michael was visibly shaken, unshaved, and rattled more than normal.

I was surprised to see Evan wearing a helmet.

I offered my arms out to hold him and calm him down. He reached out for me and it felt good with him in my arms. My instincts said it was a definite connection. I couldn't figure out what kind, but it was special.

"Oh, hi, how'd things go?" Michael said.

"Okay." I didn't feel like sharing anything with him and still felt angry inside.

"They are all on time and healthy. Crap, I forgot the other ultrasound pictures for you guys. I left them at home."

"Don't worry, we'll get them later."

"Is Evan okay? Why is he wearing a helmet?"

"It's for babies who have flat head syndrome. The helmet helps reform their heads back into shape over time. We just got it for him. It was quite expensive."

I didn't know what flat head syndrome meant, but I was concerned and filled with questions wondering why the back of his head was flat. Did they not pick him up or move him around enough? Did they leave him to cry on his back or neglect him?

Okay, Susan, back off. He's not your baby, I thought. I imagined giving myself real space and backed up a few inches to think. Evan grabbed at my lips.

"Jackie told me that Lauren gave us a referral for a high-risk baby doctor, Dr. Kazman, and she wants me to make sure you call the reduction specialist to make the appointment for the reduction. We have to do this soon." He got up from the sofa without flinching, saying it all so nonchalantly.

I was still processing what he said and I couldn't believe it. The words, "We have to do this soon" stayed in my mind.

"We?" I almost spit out the single word. "We?" I gasped.

Now I was more than angry. We hadn't even talked about it.

Well, fuck, guess what? I thought. It's my body, and I will do what I need to do with my own body, but this came out instead, "You know, Michael, it's really not a good time for me right now. I may regret anything I say to you. We'll have to talk about this later, okay?"

"Well, it needs to be done. We don't want three babies," he said. He put his arms out for Evan and I handed him back.

I drove aimlessly home, not a tear in my eye. I didn't remember the drive.

After my very long visit to the specialist that day, I waited two long hours for a five minute visit with the doctor who was going to do the reduction. I called the only person who would listen and maybe change my mind about going ahead with the reduction; Adam. I was sure because of his religion he would be against it. I wanted someone to say, "Don't do it." Whose choice was it anyway? I was so confused.

"So what are you going to do, have the reduction?" Adam asked. I heard the same comforting voice that had calmed me so many times before.

"I don't know," I said. "The doctor told me it was highly recommended that I should consider selective reduction even though all three are healthy."

Silence filled our conversation. He was the only man I ever talked to where silence felt perfect. It went on for more than a few minutes.

"What do the parents want?" he asked in his pastor's voice.

"They want me to reduce. They don't want three babies, even after I pleaded to let me carry them."

"What do you want?"

"I want to be left alone, I want someone to tell me not to do it. I don't want to have to choose. The ironic thing here is that it's not my choice because I'm not the parent, but it's my body. I feel like I need to protect them all. I'm not sure I can do this, Adam."

"I wish I could hold you," he said.

"I wish you could, too," I whimpered. "Last week when you held me, it was wonderful. By the way, you make me feel so beautiful."

"You are."

"It was so nice seeing you again after Evan was born. I'm not sure why I keep coming back to you, but being with you makes me feel alive again."

"Me too," he said softly.

I sighed long and heavily. "I've already had the amnio so the specialist can determine viability, and now it's scheduled for Friday. It's the last day, Adam. We can't do it any other time, and I don't want to do it," I said rocking my body back and forth slowly. "I'm finally done with the hormone shots. My butt was completely numb from the top of my side all the way down my right leg. But this will be worse. I don't know much about the procedure, but I know what ultimately happens."

"What happens?" he asked boldly.

I knew he would ask. I almost couldn't say it, but I felt it was safe with him. "They put a long needle through my pregnant navel and then the doctor puts potassium chloride solution into the needle. They inject it into the heart of the fetus to make it stop beating." I felt my face, body, and voice go numb telling him what would happen. My stomach felt like it was tied in knots, and then I remembered his faith and my lack thereof in his very strict Baptist God. I hoped his faith would give me strength.

I believed in a higher truth, a higher power, and something more than myself, but not like his God with a heaven and a hell. I thought about the many endless discussions about our gods while lying together sharing our thoughts.

I never set foot in a church until I was almost fifteen; I went with a caring friend who "saved me." I questioned his strict Baptist faith. There were so many rules of do this, don't do that. When I married Robert, I had to become a Catholic or we couldn't be married in the Catholic Church. I questioned that, too. I felt like you could believe in one faith, but there were so many limitations. What about love? Does the almighty God Adam believes in choose one religion over another, or does he love all humans? I wondered. All I knew was whatever higher power I believed in surrounded me with unconditional love.

"Sometimes I'm not sure why I ever became a surrogate mother," I finally said. It just didn't seem right to take one life away just because there are too many. I kept hoping they would change their minds, but now I wasn't sure they wanted any of the babies at all.

"I don't understand it. Things have changed so much," I said.

"You are going to have to do what you have to do, Susan. Think about your boys first. You are their mother and they need you. Don't try to understand it, because you can't change it now." He hit on the most loving, cherished, important part of my life—my boys.

I saw Adam's office in my mind the last time I was there. Family pictures in the background with no office window. Loads of books everywhere. I pictured where the books might have been, who borrowed them, who'd read them, and how many times tears hit the pages and altered the smell. I wished there was a book about what I was going through.

"Yeah, I know," I said. "The boys are my first priority. I don't want to put my life on the line, because I need to be here for them." It was the only thing I was sure of. I needed to be in this world for my boys.

"Yes," he said.

"Will you think less of me if I let it happen?"

He didn't hesitate. "No, no I won't. You know I pray for you all the time, and for, well, myself," he said solemnly. "No one is perfect and some things, well some things just happen in life, and you'll never know why."

He spared me the religious talk, thank God. He didn't talk me out of it, which I was sure he might try, or at least I was hoping he'd try.

Lauren called a few days later to tell me she and Tracey wouldn't be able to come with me to the reduction. Early on, they said they'd always be there for me, but apparently neither one was available on that Friday. They knew damn well I had to have it that day. Lauren told me I could have one support person with me during the procedure. I couldn't think of anyone who would want to be with me for this. Even I didn't want to be involved.

I thought of Terrie, but I couldn't ask her. I thought it would hurt her to no end and I felt I had to protect her. There was only one person in my life who I knew could endure more pain than me and handle being with me. My mother.

My mother and I had been through a lot together. But it wasn't until I told her about the childhood abuse I suffered through that we really got to know each other. I was thirty-five years old when I told her. Once I was able to admit to myself that it actually happened, all I could think of was why she didn't help me. Or whether she even knew about it. If I'd asked those questions before I got therapy, before I knew how to express myself effectively, I'm sure our discussion wouldn't have gone as well as it did. I remember our conversation going like this.

"You were what?" she said sitting in her favorite soft, brown, upholstered rocking chair. It was the most uncomfortable I'd ever seen my mom in that chair. And I was stronger than I'd ever been trying to bring the truth out into the open.

"I was mentally, emotionally, and sexually abused for years by your husband Donald, my stepfather Mom." She was across the room, but I saw the discomfort in her body, in her face.

"I was raped at a party when I was sixteen," she said. I was sitting on the blue and light brown paisley couch and my mouth fell open wide at this this news. This only added to my discomfort. I realized I was learning about my mother for the first time in my life. She was openly sharing with me. The mother-daughter connection was there but it was different, we were talking like grown women. I was being completely vulnerable, more than I'd ever been with her, and she with me. It was a start.

The therapist I was seeing at the time was my guardian angel. She asked me how I thought my mother would react when I confessed my past to her. "She'll probably say she didn't know about it, and then she'll ask what happened," I told her. And that's exactly what she said.

"That's awful," I managed to say.

"Yes, it was. I never told anyone else because I was ashamed."

"I know that feeling, Mom." I moved up on the couch.

"What happened?" she asked as she crossed her arms.

"I don't think it's important what happened, except for the fact it happened," I said. My therapist helped me say what was important to say because I didn't want to go into the details. It didn't matter and there were years of painful blocks I didn't remember.

"I always knew something wasn't right," she said. "I'm sorry, Susan, sorry I couldn't be the mother you needed. I'm sorry I was drunk all the time."

It meant everything to me to hear those words. I finally was getting to know my mother in my thirties. I felt so grateful inside that we could sit and talk.

I cried, she cried, and then we met in the middle and hugged for a very long time.

Thank goodness I was ready for it, because shame still had a hold of me. It was holding on tight and wouldn't let go until years later as I worked through a lot of anguish.

That day marked a new day for us to start over as mother and daughter. I was able to say all of the things my heart knew, many memories of my childhood. Our relationship grew deep.

Now it was time to share the horrible news with her that I had decided to fulfill Michael and Jackie's wishes to have the reduction. I wanted her to be with me and hoped she would.

"Oh, honey," she said when I asked.

"Mom, I wouldn't ask if I didn't need you. I can do it myself, but I would rather have you there to hold my hand." I felt sick to my stomach.

"I'll be there for you, but have you asked them if you can carry all three?"

"I have two doctors saying it's in the best interest for me and the babies. I can't fight this, Mom. I don't have the support of the intended parents, and if God forbid anything happened to me or I ended up on bed rest, no one would take care of the boys or my daycare, and I wouldn't have support because Jackie isn't on board with multiples. It could turn out to be a contractual nightmare because the language isn't specific in the contract about having too many babies."

There was a long silence.

"They're acting weird, Mom, just weird. I can't explain it, but something is going on with Michael and Jackie."

"Okay, I'll be there, but women have triplets all the time."

"I know, Mom, but I'm not willing to risk the situation and leave the boys without a mother if I have any complications. You and I know anything can happen and it's highly probable with triplets. Especially bed rest."

"This is abortion, Susan."

"It is, but isn't. It is abortion in utero if you absolutely want to use that word, but in fact, it is reduction of a fetus because I will still be pregnant after one is reduced. That's why they call it *selective reduction.* The whole pregnancy is not aborted."

She was silent. I wondered if she might change her mind about being with me.

"It doesn't make me feel any better, if that is what you want to know. I feel awful," I said solemnly.

The voice inside my head said, "Don't let it happen." It rattled and vibrated my brain with echoes of death, of ghosts, and cobwebs that lived there from past pain I'd accumulated in my life. I had control over my own body and because of that, it was my choice too. It would not define me, but it was something I had to live with for the rest of my life. It was still my final choice regardless of what anyone said.

This I knew to be true.

I was thirteen weeks and six days pregnant on June 23, 2001. It was time.

14

Little One

The huge, gray and white room was located in the wing of an old hospital quite a distance from the main hospital. A seven-foot-long, thin table sat in the middle of the room with two monitors on each side. I looked up at the high ceiling at what used to be white square panels, seeing some stained yellow with light brown circular, blotted spots. The room felt sterile, cold, and chilling with its hard, fluorescent lighting. I stood there in a blue and white hospital gown, barefoot and holding a white plastic bag of my belongings.

"You can put your things over there," the nurse said, pointing to a cubby by the side door as she came into the room. "Did you take everything off?"

"Yes." My hands were ice cold, so I lodged them under the pits of my arms, folding them up into myself.

She reached for the bag of clothes, and I opened my arm to hand it to her. She smiled. "Jewelry, too?"

"Yeah," I said half smiling and then folded my arm back up.

"How far along are you today, Susan?"

"Thirteen weeks, six days." I looked around the room.

"Your age?"

"Thirty-nine." I felt way too old to be in this position. I

looked into her dark, friendly eyes. Her makeup looked dramatic and perfect.

"Feeling okay?" She started to write in my chart.

"I'm okay," I lied. "I'm a little scared because I don't know how this is going to happen, but I do know I don't want to see it." I pointed to the monitors by the table.

"You'll be fine, don't worry. You don't have to watch. The doctor and ultrasound technician need to see what's going on inside your womb during the reduction." She put my chart down then pushed her shoulder-length brown hair up into a perfect bun on top of her head, pulling it into her surgical bonnet.

"Isn't it too late to be doing this?" I hoped she would realize the gross error that was about to happen because I was more than twelve weeks pregnant and all the babies were healthy. I wanted someone to notice.

"Unfortunately, they like to do it as late as possible. Any time between 12 and 14 weeks is better because the fetus is bigger and it is easier to manipulate the instruments."

I still felt like running away to save them all. "When will I be put out?" I asked.

"You won't have any medication, Susan," she explained. "You are pregnant with three now and will still be pregnant with two when it's over. We don't want to harm the other ones."

I didn't want to harm any of them.

"We do this all the time without anesthesia," she said reassuringly.

I stared at her, half believing she was lying, and my voice came louder. "Nothing? I won't need anything and I stay awake the whole time?"

"No, you won't need anything." She shook her head. "IVF isn't an exact science and sometimes you end up with more than you should carry. The risk with multiples is high for the mother and the child, which is why we do reduction."

She sounded like my doctor. I looked down at the floor. I

couldn't believe they weren't going to put me out. I let out a weighted sigh. I wanted to be sedated, drugged, or unconscious. I didn't want to feel anything, physically or mentally. I couldn't even believe I was there.

"You'll need to lie flat on your back on this table," she said as she pointed to the operating table.

I walked over and put my hand on the top. The surface felt hard and I would have to lie flat on my back, the worst position for a pregnant woman.

She covered the ultrasound screen closest to my view with blue sterilized lap paper and left the other one open for the doctor. "We've seen some horror stories with women trying to carry more babies than they should and it's sad because it can be prevented with selective reduction. That's why Dr. Taylor does this procedure, to limit pre-term labor and keep babies safe in-utero so they can be born healthy. He specializes in high-risk. That's why you waited so long in the waiting room. He's always busy helping someone in distress."

"How does the doctor choose which one?"

"The doctor will take the one weakest one, with less am-niotic fluid, or the one in a bad position in your womb. He'll confirm it before he starts. It's a lot like the amniocentesis you had at your last visit here, only this time with a bigger needle that goes inside your navel. You'll feel a little prick and it's over once the needle full of chemical is injected into the heart and it stops beating."

My heart sank. "What happens to the…"

"It's reabsorbed into your body during the pregnancy."

"How long before that happens?"

"It depends on the person. Okay, you need to get up here and lie down. The doctor will be in soon. I'll get you a blanket." She walked out of the room.

The lights over my head were so bright they hurt my eyes and I couldn't see. Tears kept forming puddles in my eyes, making my vision murky. I whisked them away and climbed up onto the table and sat. I didn't want to lie down until I had to.

I thought about begging Michael and Jackie one last time. They were supposed to be in the waiting room, but I didn't care if they showed up or not. They only wanted twins and were insistent about the reduction.

The nurse came back. "Okay, lie down please." She patted the table above my back.

I laid down and the thin paper shredded as I pulled my heavy pregnant body up trying to get comfortable, but there was no comfort on the table. The paper melded to my sticky body, and pieces of it were all over my backside. I wiped my eyes and it stuck to my face.

"Don't worry about that paper. We don't really need it," she said.

I wondered where the extra blanket was but didn't say anything. I felt awkward lying flat on my back with my tummy up and unprotected. The nurse pulled up a leather strap that was fixed to the underside on the four corners of the table. I thought, *No, this is not happening. She is not going to strap down my arms and legs.* She took my right leg and fixed it into the leather buckle.

"What are you doing? Is this really necessary?" I felt odd and threatened.

"Yes, it's our medical protocol, sorry."

This is why they don't tell you what happens with this procedure, I thought. If I knew this, I wouldn't have shown up.

It felt like something out of a movie, but it was really happening to me. It didn't seem right when she took my arms and secured them to the table. The leather from the straps looked like they'd been used many times before from the stretched ring holes in the raw leather. I heard her tug on the buckle from under the table pulling it up through the loop into position, and then she reached under the table, opened a drawer, and pulled out a thin white cotton blanket.

"Only one blanket," she said. "I'll go find another one." She pulled it over my body up to my neck. My feet popped out from the bottom and I couldn't move to adjust it. I wished I had kept my socks on, but she insisted I take everything off. It was so cold. I started to shiver. I couldn't run now, I thought, and started to get anxious. I pushed against the straps with my four limbs and felt the tension weigh me down, making me feel exposed, trapped, and vulnerable, like a live specimen waiting to be dissected.

The last time I was here the doctor told me he was "letting go of one to save the other two."

Questions swam through my mind. There wasn't enough information online and the office didn't tell me a lot about it other than "one fetus will be terminated." Did I really want to know any more?

It was my body. I could demand to be let up and refuse this whole thing, but what would happen if I had medical problems later? What if the babies were born prematurely? What if I lost all three because of problems later and was bedridden for months? Who would take care of my kids or daycare? What if Michael and Jackie sued me for breaching the contract and not following what the contract deemed "medically necessary?"

Everyone said two would be better, safer. I had to let this happen.

I thought of the last ultrasound. All three were healthy, thriving, and bouncing happily around in my womb.

Cold set into my bones and I shivered with fear and doubt so thick I could barely breathe. Feeling helpless and trapped, I ordered my body to stop shivering, but it wouldn't, and then I started to cry.

The nurse walked back in with the ultrasound tech and behind her came my mother, who stood by the door looking at me and then at the nurse. Reading her face, I knew she didn't know where to sit and she did not want to be with me to witness this.

"You will sit here on this stool, and the doctor will be on

the other side over there," the nurse said and pointed to the other side of me. My mom went to her seat, sat down, and whispered in my ear, "I don't agree with what is happening, Susan, but I want to be here for you."

I didn't know what to say because I was sure whatever I said wouldn't come out right, so I said nothing. Goddammit, couldn't she have just said she was here for me? I knew she didn't agree with it.

She put her hand on my shoulder. "I'm always here, right here on your shoulder." She tapped it softly, again and again, which irritated me.

Dr. Taylor was one of seven doctors in the country who performed selective reduction. His main business was high risk OB-GYN and our only visit was rushed. He had been busy and I waited three hours to be seen. We didn't exactly hit it off.

He came in pushing back his long, bushy, black and gray straggly eyebrows up over his eyes and they went clear to his forehead. He looked around the room, bewildered.

"Marjorie, where is the machine?" he said, annoyed.

The ultrasound technician pointed to the other side of the room. "Over there, doctor."

"Why aren't you ready yet?"

She didn't answer and sighed like she wasn't there.

He walked over to the machine and wheeled it in front of her. "Let's get going here." He pushed his hands over the top of his head.

"Yes, doctor."

He pointed at my mother. "You her mother?"

"Yes," my mother whispered through the surgical mask covering her mouth.

"If it makes any difference to you, medically speaking, she's doing the right thing."

She bowed her head as if to acknowledge what he said, and then reached down to touch my hand and felt the strap. "What is this?"

"Straps, chains, they don't want me to escape," I said, not joking. It felt as if my voice was stifled, stuffed down just like my shame.

She fumbled around in her chair and rolled her eyes showing her disapproval.

The doctor went out and came back with someone following him. I popped my head up and saw Michael and Jackie.

"I told you, it is my final answer. I will not reduce because of sex," Dr. Taylor said standing eye to eye with Jackie.

"Doctor, you don't understand. We would like to choose if you know the sexes," she bantered, touching her mouth mask. I imagined it stuffed in her mouth so she couldn't talk at all.

"I do understand. You do not understand that we do not base our decision to terminate on sex. We will choose the weakest one," Dr. Taylor said, remaining professional. I looked again to make sure it was the same doctor.

"You will not play God here," he said sternly. "It is a reduction so you will have two healthy babies that will go to term."

Everyone looked at each other without speaking.

"Now, please, both of you leave my operating room," he said.

They looked over at me and then at my mom.

I felt embarrassed for them. What a thing to ask. Did they have a secret agenda based on the sex of the babies? As far as I knew they didn't even know what the sexes were and neither did I. We did an amniocentesis a few days before, so I was sure the doctor had the information because he had checked them for abnormalities as well.

My mom looked down at me and let out a heavy sigh into my face. Her hot breath hit my nose and I closed my eyes.

"I don't care what they say, that isn't how I do things," Dr. Taylor said. "I will choose the weakest one as of this date."

I started to cry again. I couldn't help it. It seemed the only thing to do. I felt sad with guilt and doubt clouding my judgment.

The thought crossed my mind that I wanted Michael and

Jackie to see this so they would know what happens when they decide to terminate one of their children. I wanted them to feel it and hurt like I was. I felt like a puppet, doing everything everyone else wanted. I looked at my pregnant belly and felt like I might lose the whole pregnancy.

I thought about my closest friend, Terrie, being with me instead of my mom. I felt she would never forgive me if she had to witness this. It was too much for anyone to have to go through. I felt fortunate to have my mom with me. Otherwise, I would have been alone.

Everything I believed about surrogacy started to fall apart, little by little. It wasn't supposed to be this way.

Dr. Taylor put on his mask and the nurse slid on his gloves. He lifted a needle as large as a ruler from the table. I stiffened and got dizzy wondering how he felt about what he does. Had he totally desensitized himself? I'm sure he thought for medical reasons that two is healthier than three.

I couldn't get comfortable and wanted to curl up on my left side into a fetal position and be left alone, but I knew I had to be still. I tried to think of something else, but couldn't.

He pushed the long needle into a round metal rod after the nurse filled it with potassium chloride. When he got closer to me, I started to convulse with cold so hard my teeth chattered.

The nurse covered my belly with betadine using an extra-large cotton swab. I felt it drip down my sides, making me colder. I started to shiver harder and I couldn't think straight. Fear took over and I couldn't think of anything other than just that. Fear.

I heard my mom say, "You okay, honey?"

I didn't know how to answer, so I looked up at her childlike, pathetic, and fearful. She grabbed my hand and squeezed it with motherly support. Tears rolled down her cheeks.

Dr. Taylor plunged the long needle into my abdomen. It felt like a foreign object invading my body, oddly painless. A slight numbing shock entered my core.

My mom held my head and her warm tears fell onto my face. She moved her head forward, then side to side to wipe her tears. Her head hit the blue drape covering the monitor, and it floated to the ground giving a full view of everything inside my womb.

I looked over and saw three little honeycombed shaped sacs inside the monitor, an umbilical cord inside each with tiny little legs, arms, and head with eyes, ears, nose, and mouth. And the hearts in clear view.

I started to sob into my mother's arms and turned away from the monitor, my heart aching. "I'm soooo sorry...I'm sorry," I whimpered. "Can't I please be put out somehow? Anything? Why aren't you putting me out?" The doctor didn't respond. The nurse shook her head.

"I told you," she said. "We can't give you anything, it is minimal pain, I'm sorry."

She looked up to see the drape had fallen. The light hit her pretty dark eyes, and I saw her forehead wrinkle in concern above her mask. She couldn't put it back up because she was assisting the doctor, so she put her head back down.

"You don't need to see this, Susan," my mom whispered. She covered my eyes with her open hand, but I jerked my head away, my arms and legs still strapped down.

I remembered the time she tried to shield me from seeing the death of our seven-week old kittens at the hands of my stepfather Donald, after I'd witnessed the kittens being born. I was eleven when he stuffed them all into a grocery bag and held it under the muffler of our Impala. "I have too many mouths to feed," he said. My little body tried to stop him, but I was powerless. My mother grabbed me away and put her hands over my eyes stopping me from seeing him go into the garage. The high-pitched mews were unbearable, and then nothing, no sounds as the noxious smell poured into the house from the garage. I cried for months because I was scared to death of him. He was showing me he could and would kill if I ever told the secret.

"I'm okay, Mom," I lied again, trying to be strong, but I felt fragile and weak as tears streamed down my face. I tried to wipe them away, but the strap restricted my movement to less than half an inch. I looked up to see the needle probing the little fetal sac and turned away again.

I couldn't look.

I felt so responsible. This little one wouldn't be born like the other two. My gown was soaked with tears and I couldn't breathe. I saw the little fetus move away from the needle, sensing the danger. The other two also moved away from the middle. I felt a twinge of pain shoot through me and my body flinched from head to toe.

Dr. Taylor pulled the needle back and moved some levers from the rod, struggling with it, as it seemed to push the fetus away with air from the needle. It didn't look like he hit it. I couldn't be sure that he penetrated the body with the needle. He pulled up and backed away from the table like he missed it.

His face looked surprised.

I saw it still moving, struggling. My mind shouted, "Stop!" I might have shouted it out loud, but words wouldn't undo what happened. My mom's tears fell onto my cheeks drop by drop as she held me close and we both turned away from the monitor sobbing.

Dr. Taylor and the nurse stepped away from the table and stared at the screen, waiting and watching. I could feel the heavy breathing from the other side of the table, and saw their chests moving in and out. The betadine all over my belly permeated my sense of smell, and painfully dripped a trickle down my sides. I wanted to scratch it away.

The horror was that the heartbeat didn't stop. I could tell by their faces.

"Isn't it supposed to stop?" I pleaded.

Dr. Taylor looked at me and then stepped to the table behind him and grabbed some tools. Everything I read about what would happen did not happen.

Did it move too quickly making him miss the heart? Was the medication the right dose? Did he screw it up? Did he hit the amniotic sac but miss the heart? These were all questions that would never be answered because I didn't know anything about the procedure and then never asked. Was it better that I didn't know?

This little one was fighting. I could see the anguish in the doctor's eyes. He dropped his arms to his sides and backed away. It seemed he didn't know what to do.

The tension in the room felt deathly dark and uncomfortable, like it was everywhere and none of us knew what to do next, looking at one another.

"Help it," I said weakly. I looked back at the screen. Why did I have to look up? I didn't want to see it, yet I felt like I needed to witness it and felt responsible for my part. I didn't think I'd ever recover from what I let happen.

The dark-haired nurse with large eyes looked over at Dr. Taylor from across the table.

I never stopped crying like a baby into my mother's arms.

Still nothing happened while the doctor waited. I glared numbly at the screen, not wanting to look, but I did. It was like seeing a car accident on the side of the road—staring and wanting to help, but helpless.

Dr. Taylor grabbed a large plastic syringe and connected it to what looked like the rod that was buried in my navel and started to suction up something.

What was he doing?

I screamed out in agony as he suctioned up what I believed to be the amniotic fluid from the fetus, pulling the salty life-sustaining fluid up through the placenta, and up through my veins that I shared with the fetus. Was I feeling what it felt? I heard myself screaming and felt sheer burning pain like nothing I'd ever felt before. I screamed as loud as I could, wailing and scared for my own life.

I tried not to move, but it was impossible, so I howled in

pain knowing the fetus must have been in pain too, which made me cry harder.

The doctor moved fast.

My head was straight up off the hard table. I leaned forward with my arms and legs strapped down. Fluid swished up through the rod into the large plastic syringe. My mind fixated on my own pain as Dr. Taylor reloaded and dumped the fluid into a stainless steel bowl.

My guttural screams could surely be heard for miles and were embedded in the yellow- and brown-stained ceiling above. He stopped and my body remembered the pain and went numb, then he pulled the rod with the needle and syringe out of my abdomen looking at me, surprised at my pain. My first thought was he had never done this before.

I heard my own whimpering. It was torture and I could not figure out what happened and why.

I looked over at the nurse who looked away. I looked at the doctor and he wouldn't look at me. I looked over at the ultrasound tech and she had her head down, still invisible.

My body was a whirlwind of radiating, numbing pain, and my mind was confused. Was the sodium potassium getting into my own system? Is that what I felt or was it the amniotic fluid that burned? If it came from the amniotic sac, then it came up through my body. I lay cold and not shivering, numb and frozen on the hard table.

I wanted it to end. I prayed for the little fetus to let go. My head fell back with a thump.

My mom stepped back looking like she wanted to stop the whole thing, yet she too was helpless.

Breathe. Just continue to breathe, I thought.

This was not the way it was supposed to happen. I could see the surprise on the faces of the nurse and technician. There wasn't a dry face in the room, except for Dr. Taylor, whose face was sweating profusely. His surgical cap was drenched.

We all looked up at the screen as the little fetus retracted and shriveled up. We couldn't see a heartbeat.

"We're done here," the doctor said without energy.

All of life seemed to stand still.

"Don't move, we'll check it again in five minutes," he said to me.

He left the room and the nurse followed.

"Please take these straps off, I can't breathe." The nurse looked at the ultrasound tech and she came to my side.

"We can't yet, we will as soon as we can."

She walked over to the open monitor by me and covered the screen with new blue paper. I lay there, a lifeless pregnant woman with twins and a dead fetus in my womb. My mom had her head down to the side of my shoulder and her hands up as if praying. I'd never seen her do that in all of my life.

The whole procedure from start to end took what seemed like the whole day. Somewhere between the end and making it back to the car, I was in a state of shock. It felt like I was going to lose the other two babies if I didn't walk slowly, like everything was going to drop through and down to the bottom of my body.

A gloomy June wind howled briskly above the tall trees and echoed between the tall buildings as I left. Everything around me was moving in slow motion and I didn't hear what anyone said, all words sounded muffled.

A thought rang through my head. Is this what it feels like before you have a nervous breakdown? Could this really be happening to me? I didn't want to be crazy. It must have been for my own self-protection.

My last memory of that day was getting into the car as I plopped down on the passenger seat and put my hand over my heart. When I closed the door, the last wind whipped up into the car, and through what felt like my empty soul.

15

More Surprises

The doctor ordered two days of strict bed rest. My mother was scheduled to go home the day after the reduction. Michael and Jackie were instructed by Tracey and Lauren to hire help for me on Sunday, but instead of hiring help, they decided to come to my house themselves and help. I didn't know any of this until they showed up at my front door Sunday morning.

"Susan! Where do you keep the milk? I don't see it in the refrigerator," Jackie yelled from the top of nine stairs while I rested downstairs in our split-level home. Michael was watching cartoons with the boys in the living room, and Terrie was working in her room. Sunday was my regular shopping day, so I knew I didn't have any milk in the house. I cringed at the thought of Michael and Jackie picking out my groceries. I crept up the stairs holding my mid-section feeling protective. I looked at Jackie and saw something I hadn't seen before. She was carefree, almost too calm, like she wasn't worried about me, or the twins. I wondered what was up.

During the third or fourth hour of me going up and down the stairs to take care of people, and answer Jackie's questions I'd had enough. Jackie came down the stairs as I was going up again and asked, "How are you feeling?"

"I'm really tired and very achy. I don't feel good about this pregnancy right now, and I'm a little worried," I said, shaking and weak. I wanted to tell her that something was missing from my body. Something died inside of me and it was still there, but not there. I was incredibly sad about it. I wanted her to acknowledge there was a dead baby floating in my womb and I was angry with her and Michael, but instead, I just stared at her.

"Well, if it makes you feel any better Michael and I talked, and if you want to abort the other two, it's okay with us. This will do it naturally." She pointed to the stairs.

I stopped on the middle stair and stared into her face, seeing a person moving around as a human being with what seemed like no heart in her body. Stunned, I found the strength to say, "So, this is what you are doing. You don't want any of them, do you?"

"No, it's not that, but maybe it's just not the time. We want them, but right now things have changed with Michael and me, and we are re-evaluating whether more kids would be good for us right now. Evan is so much work and very expensive," she said.

I heard Evan crying upstairs.

"You need to leave. Now." My blood turned to a low simmer.

"What?" she said. I didn't know what else to say to her. I whispered under my breath. *I thought I trusted these people.* I lifted my head and met her eyes. Apparently she didn't hear, or she chose to ignore what I said, so I said it again in a voice she could hear without drawing attention to the boys upstairs. "Please go, just go. I don't need your kind of help."

She turned away with a look that said she was pleased to leave. She didn't want to be helping me at my house. "I will never abort this pregnancy, so don't ever ask me to again," I added with my teeth clenched in the meanest voice I could muster as she went up the last few stairs.

I was so angry.

I reminded myself that these were legally their babies, but there was no way in hell I would abort the other two. The intention to bring them into the world was Michael and Jackie's, and now they didn't want any of them? It didn't add up. I was confused. We still had a long way to go with the pregnancy. I was just shy of fourteen weeks.

She hit the top of the stairs, walked over to Michael sitting on the couch and said, "Let's go."

He looked up, surprised, and followed her out the door holding the baby.

I didn't want to make a scene in front of the boys, but I felt relieved the moment they were out the front door. I heard what she said, and I saw how she wanted me to end the pregnancy but I still didn't believe her! How could they not want their own babies—full siblings to Evan? I was flooded with emotions, ones I didn't know what to do with. I wanted to cry and scream at the same time.

I called the 24-hour beeper number for Lauren and Tracey to let them know what happened and didn't hear back from them until the next day. Tracey was supposed to be on call. They had given me this number for support, but there was none. I wondered why I even had an agency. Lauren returned my call the next day and said, "I'll take care of it."

Weeks passed, and I didn't hear back from Michael, Jackie, or the agency. I tried hard to return back to my normal life, but I couldn't stop thinking about what happened. I'd taken my grief and guilt and buried it deep down inside, like I always did. It was all I knew how to do.

On the first Monday in August 2001 I walked out to the mailbox to pick up our mail on one of the warmest days we'd had in a long time. I was miserably hot. I pulled the mail out, shuffled through it, and saw an envelope from my medical insurance company that had a "Past Due" notice on the outside. I ripped it open and my HIPAA rights and a bill came tumbling out. What did I miss? This was supposed to be paid directly by the agency. The notice said if I didn't pay immediately, my medical insurance would be cancelled. I called the agency.

"You haven't heard from Michael and Jackie?" Tracey asked.

"No. What's going on? Why am I suddenly receiving collection notices?"

"Oh, I don't know. Those should have been paid. I'll look into it."

She knew I shouldn't receive these notices, and I sensed something in her voice that she wasn't telling me. All of the bills had been going directly to the agency, and if I did receive one, it was not a "Past Due" one.

"Ok, let me know what you find as soon as possible," I said. "I'm not calling Michael or Jackie because of what happened when they were here last. It's sad our journey is turning out like this, but I don't want to deal with them right now." I put down the notice and wondered what was going on. I grabbed my checkbook to pay my medical insurance because I didn't want it to be cancelled.

Weeks passed and I started receiving other collection notices from the specialists and ultrasound bills for our 20% due after insurance paid. One bill was from the hospital where I had the reduction. It read printed in red ink, "Pay $2,523.00 Now!"

I called the agency again.

"Tracey, what the fuck? This is not a good reflection on my credit. I'm trying to keep it as clean as possible, especially after the divorce. This bill needs to be paid as soon as possible, like now! What is going on?"

"We need to talk to you, it's important," she said.

"What? Tell me right now on the phone. What could be so important?"

"No, we need to talk to you in person. Together. Lauren and myself."

I couldn't imagine what she would tell me, and I had no clue why it had to be in person. It had to be a financial concern, I thought. What happened?

They showed up at my house the next day, a Friday. The kids were at school and the house was quiet. They sat on the couch together anticipating something they didn't want to tell me. Tracey's Angel perfume was strangling me and making me nauseous. I sat at the table to give myself some distance from her and so we could go over the bills. Lauren asked me to sit down on the couch with them, so I got up and walked slowly over to the couch. I felt sick from the perfume and opened the window by the couch for some air.

They both took a deep breath and said together, "Michael and Jackie do not want the twins."

Lauren added, "They are divorcing and want out of the contract. Jackie claims that Michael is suffering from bipolar disorder."

"What?"

All I could hear was "don't want twins" and then "bipolar." All I could think of was they can't do that. It's not possible.

"What am I going to do?" I said confused. My hearing felt muffled.

"We don't know," Tracey replied. "And there is no money left in the trust to pay any more bills."

"What?" It now felt like a nightmare that I could not wake up from. It was all so overwhelming; it didn't hit me earlier like it did this time. Three *big* things: don't want twins, psychological issues, and no money in the trust. It's a good thing I was sitting down, because I felt sick and dizzy.

"Weren't you guys supposed to take care of all the financials before we started our journey? The trust should have been fully funded like it was the first time."

"Yes, but Tracey offered progress payments this time instead of getting it all up front before we began. She trusted them because of our first journey. They were supposed to pay at quarterly intervals and now they are not paying at all," Lauren said.

"Great, make it all my fault," Tracey replied angrily and slouched back on the couch.

"No, they can't do this," I said gearing myself up. "We have a signed, tight contract. They can't just get out of it. It's a breach of contract on their part if they do."

I couldn't breathe and my heart raced. "What are we going to do?" My mind wouldn't let the thought go. "What will happen?"

"We don't know," Lauren said. She sounded exhausted. "We've talked to our personal attorneys, but they don't specialize in surrogacy, and both the attorneys we used to sign contracts for your side and for their side won't return our calls. Both of them told us we have to hire separate surrogacy attorneys. They are only responsible for drafting and signing the contracts, not for additional services."

I didn't know what to think about the situation, but one thing I did know was that I had to take care of the twins.

"So, wait. What? The attorneys that helped us in the beginning won't talk to you or me?"

"Right. They said it was a conflict of interest and they couldn't talk or give advice to either party," Tracey said.

"How long have you known this?" I said.

Silence.

I nodded. "So, for a while?" I sighed in disbelief. *Don't want the twins* continued to ring in my ears.

"We didn't want to tell you right after the reduction, and when Dr. Taylor told us you were carrying a healthy boy and girl we thought they might come around because of the twins," Lauren said. "We were worried for your health and the pregnancy, Susan."

"They might still come around, Susan," Tracey whined. "Don't let go of that thought."

"What? I'm supposed to sit around and wait for them to

come around? I can't believe you said that. How am I going to go through this pregnancy without medical insurance or the bills being paid? You guys have to do something."

"What do you want us to do?" Tracey asked.

"You got me... *us* into this, and you need to get us out."

I got up from the couch slowly. I started to pace wondering what I was going to do, and then I sat back down.

"Okay, well, we need to leave now," Lauren said. "Think about it, Susan, and we'll work it out somehow." She headed for the door and motioned for Tracey to follow her.

After they left, I called the third party trust accountant for the surrogacy at Tracey's personal attorney's office. They told me there was $11,000 left in the trust designated as the other half of the agency fee. "Specific instructions to hold it for them, per Tracey at the agency," the woman told me.

"We're having problems and the money left in the account is to be used for medical insurance premiums and past due bills, *not* to be held for the agency fee. If anyone says otherwise, we will have more problems than we have now," I said.

Tracey called me within 10 minutes.

"Susan, you had no right to call the attorney's office and the money left in the account is for the other half of our fee."

"Not anymore," I said. "And yes, I have every right. You screwed up, Tracey, which now makes it my business."

"Well, we can't use it for your surrogacy compensation either."

"I couldn't care less about that right now, Tracey. They've only made a few small contract payments to me anyway. We've got more important things here to deal with. I don't appreciate being lied to about the funds left in the trust. If we are going to work together, we have to trust each other," I said, only half believing I could ever trust her again, but I didn't have any choice.

"Okay, send the overdue bills to me, and I'll get them paid," she said.

"Fine. I'm still shocked to hear that Michael has psychological problems and even more upset that it is now my problem. Did you guys do any kind of background check on Michael and Jackie? Why did you only screen me?"

"Because every agency does the same thing, Susan. We only screen the surrogate mother."

"It's unfair to do it that way, Tracey, and it's probably because they're holding the checkbook right?"

"It doesn't ever happen this way. No one has ever walked away from a surrogacy arrangement and their own children. This is the first time this kind of thing has ever happened that we know of, and we've been checking around with those who know."

I could not believe it all was happening. I put my hand on my growing belly thinking of two healthy babies in my womb, abandoned before they were even born. It wasn't going to happen, not on my watch. I started to feel my instinctive, maternal strength bubbling up.

I was so angry the agency had such a high fee. Their fee matched what I received as a surrogate mother, and they didn't carry the baby for nine months! I thought all agencies were a shield and protective guide to help the intended parents and the surrogate through the process. They were not any of guide and they clearly didn't know what they were doing. At the very best, they were matchmakers. At the same time, I didn't want to alienate them because I might need their help later on. Later that evening, I realized there was no protecting anyone from anything. Even with a solid contract, people can change their minds anytime they want, for whatever reason.

When I woke the next morning it occurred to me that I needed to start building a legal case. I knew enough to know the one with the most accurate paperwork usually wins. Not always, of course, but it was good to have a daily accounting and look into possible legal avenues. It was clear no one was going to help me, so I knew it was up to me.

I started to document everything and thankfully had already been keeping a daily diary. I had a yearly fold-out calendar for 2001, listing the first important fact, the transfer date of the embryos. April 8th which was Palm Sunday. I neatly wrote all of my medical appointments on one page and listed who was there with specific dates. When I was out of the house, I wrote on paper napkins, box lids, anything I could find to write details to help my case—one I wasn't even sure I had.

Michael and Jackie might change their minds, I thought over and over again, but if they didn't, I needed to be prepared. Questions started swimming in my head. Do I need an attorney? Who should I call? I tried to call Michael and Jackie again to work things out, but neither of them returned my calls. "Goddamn them," I mumbled. I tried to put myself in their shoes, and still kept wondering why they would do this.

One week toppled over another and my anxiety grew along with my belly. I thought about the dead fetus in my womb every day, and when I focused on it too much, I couldn't think clearly at all.

16

Legal Options

At twenty-six weeks pregnant, I decided to find an attorney and had no idea where to start. Tracey and Lauren weren't helping and they seemed more helpless than I was. I researched attorneys on the internet searching endlessly through page after page of results, trying to connect to surrogacy law to see who might represent me. There must be options. I needed to know more about the legal options, my legal options, if I had any at all.

After days of phone calls to attorneys, leaving short to lengthy messages for a call back, it was clear that this whole thing was going to be a challenge. The hardest thing I ran into was finding anyone who would believe my story. I was hung up on at least a dozen times and doubters took questionable messages. Comments like, "Oh, right. This call is ridiculous." Or, I'd get short response from many calls; "We don't do surrogacy." One woman said, "Surrogates are paid to have a child. How can you be okay with that?" Sometimes I told the whole story only to hear, "Nope, can't take that on. Can't afford to."

Click. Another one shot down. Check that one off. I pushed the telephone book off what was left of my lap, and my notes fell to the floor.

One of the last attorneys I tried was the one I wasn't sure could help because he'd made history with helping intended parents win in a legal case against their surrogate. He was the only one with surrogacy experience left on my list Richard Walton. When I first reached him on the phone, I could tell he was curious when he didn't shut me down right away.

"So, if you come to my office, you will be very pregnant with twins, and both of the intended parents do not want them, is that correct?" he said in a whimsical voice.

"Right," I said, hoping to make it to his office and place my huge pregnant body in his chair.

"Okay, well come to my office and we'll see what we can do, but you have to bring your contract. Understand?"

"Yeah, I got it," I said, happy he would talk to me. I was starting to be fed up with what felt like condescending comments. Of course I'd bring the contract; it was the only thing that was on my side.

A week later I arrived at Richard Walton's Orange County office with my contract in hand. His office looked like an old school attorney's office, vintage 1960's. Strong male influence of black leather tufted couches, square oak tables with oversized yellowing lampshades on them with odd shaped bases that were an orange-y lime-green with odd shapes rounding out the Sixties loud motif.

When his assistant walked me into his office, he stood to invite me in. *A gentleman*, I thought. He had pictures on the oak credenza behind him of what I assumed to be his wife and children. Good, he had kids, I thought. His wall reflected certificates of achievement and articles of his career with which he made precedence in the surrogacy field for intended parents, not surrogates.

"Hi, Susan, have a seat. Sorry we have to meet under these circumstances," he said holding his tie back to sit down.

"Thank you," I said hoping I'd found someone who could help us.

"You are indeed pregnant." He glanced up and down my body.

"Yes." I nodded and managed a faint smile.

"Did you bring your contract?"

"Yes." I handed it to him. "Thank you for your time, Mr. Walton."

"No, please call me Richard."

"Richard," I said warmly.

He was an average-size man with honey-colored hair parted to one side and light blue eyes that looked like beams of light reflecting the bluest sky, the kind that drew you in just from their unique color. He sat quietly scanning my twenty-eight page contract. The twins were actively kicking inside of me. Hard. I adjusted them and rubbed my tummy to calm them down. It was painfully aching. Sometimes when they kicked, it'd be so hard that I'd jump up startled at the kick from my body. It must have been an odd thing to watch if you weren't the one pregnant. I rubbed my belly again.

"Well, this is the standard contract, and from what I can see here, and if what you are saying is true, then the intended parents are in breach of this contract for non-payment, but it's a breach nonetheless."

"Yes, I suspected that, but what can I do if they don't want their babies?"

"You can't do anything. They aren't your babies and even if they are negligent parents, you can't do anything until the babies are born. It's only then after they are born, that the law recognizes them under family law. A contract is under civil law, not family law. You simply can't do anything right now unless the parents agree to do something before the twins are born. If they don't, there is nothing you can do. Your hands are basically tied, Susan."

"But, can I go for parentage once they are born?"

"You can, but you won't win. Everything in the contract is written in the intended parents' interest, not yours. My job is to fight for intended parents' rights, not a surrogate's rights. It's what surrogacy is for." His bright, soft blue eyes went serious.

"Why? Is there a surrogate attorney I can go to?"

"I don't know of any. Probably because of the Baby M case to be specific, and the one I helped on. There are no specific surrogate attorneys I know of."

"This has nothing to do with the Baby M case. This is the opposite of the Baby M case. I'm not related to the twins, and in the other case there is biology involved. So, I'm pretty screwed because I'm not holding a fat wallet, right?"

Both of us studied each other.

"They want me to send the babies to social services when they are born, and this was after I went through a selective reduction at their request," I pleaded.

"I feel for you, Susan, I really do, but if what you say is true, why wouldn't at least one of the parents want the twins? The one genetically related would be the appropriate one, the father in this case."

"I've been told he is incapable of taking care of himself, let alone twins. He is bipolar, stressed to the max, and possibly off his medications." As I heard myself say the words, I couldn't even believe my own story.

"Have you checked the grandparents or the people listed as back up in the contract?"

"Yes. The agency contacted them and said they didn't even know Michael and Jackie were trying to have children. The contract backup is Michael's brother, who has three kids of his own, and was not aware that he and his wife were listed as backup." It felt like I was pleading a case before a judge.

"You simply can't do anything right now unless the intended parents sign over their parental rights to you before the babies are born. Have they filed the pre-birth order yet?"

"No, and they have no intention to. They don't want the

twins and won't return my messages." I shrunk down in my chair with one hand on my large belly trying to get comfortable.

"I don't know how I can help you, Susan. I don't fight for surrogate rights, and my fees are probably more than you can afford." I felt low earlier from his comments, but this one brought me to an all-time low.

I wanted to cry again, but instead I thought of a reason to leave.

"Okay, well, thank you for your time." I pulled myself up from the comfy black leather chair. Richard stood. Out of curiosity I asked, "What are your fees?"

"Five thousand dollar retainer to start."

I slowly moved my head up and down. "You're right, it's more than I can afford."

I waddled to the door and looked back at him before I opened it.

"I'll just represent myself because there is no way in hell I'm letting the twins go to social services." I started to head out the door but stopped when I heard Richard's voice.

"Can I ask you if you have any intention of keeping the twins?" he asked.

"No, I can't, I mean... I never thought..." My voice trailed off and now I was definitely going to cry. I cleared my throat and said, "I never thought something like this could happen. I became a surrogate mother to help others, not make a new family for myself. I have two young boys and I'm a single mother. I went into this with the mindset that they were not mine. I just can't."

"I am sorry I can't help you, Susan."

All the way to my doctor's appointment for a checkup the next day, I felt defeated and knocked down once again, knowing full well that I would probably have no legal assistance. I didn't care I was going to do it myself if I had to. Someone would have to help eventually, I thought. The law would have to be on my side for trying to do the right thing. I thought about the life I might have saved if I'd known about this earlier. I wasn't so sure I would have had the reduction, but it didn't matter now. I made the decision and would have to live with my choice.

I saw the dead fetus on the monitor at my last doctor visit when Dr. Kazman did an ultrasound to check the babies. He was a gentle soul, and handsome for a doctor with dark wavy black hair and round rimmed glasses. He tried to move the wand quickly when we saw it, but he paused too long. I knew what was floating in my womb. I wished I hadn't seen it. He was right to try to shield me from it. Remorse. Guilt. Shame. Hate. All those feelings were surfacing again. I cried on the way out, damning myself for crying again. I was sick of crying, but the tears kept coming.

17

9/11

A few days later, on September 11, 2001, I woke up and started our day like any other school day. The boys were waking slowly and wanted to stay in bed. "Time to get up, let's go guys," I said as I tugged on the bottom of their bed covers just like I did every day. I went upstairs to start making breakfast. I felt the twins moving in my belly and around my sides with each stair. I tucked my hand low underneath my belly to push them up a little higher to keep them in place.

It was 9/11—the day the twin towers fell. I can't say how the disaster affected the world and its people, but it did. It affected me by thinking of the two boys I brought into this world already and Evan, along with the two I would soon give birth to. This world was already so wrought with the chaos of my own present reality, and now the terror outside my door. The kids' school that morning started later than usual, and everyone had the same sad look. Those who didn't know what happened learned from those of us who did, and their faces quickly turned to the same despairing look.

Later that month I reached the thirty-one weeks pregnant mark. I had swollen ankles and felt huge. Heartburn had me by the throat. Adding to my physical discomfort was the knowledge that Michael and Jackie still hadn't completed the standard pre-birth order. I was starting to feel desperate which I saw as a red flag. But, really it was a clear sign that they were not planning on becoming the parents or they would have done the pre-birth order by now. God knows I was looking for a sign.

I wanted to know if Michael and Jackie were serious about not wanting the twins. I wanted answers. They finally called. Jackie told me she was divorcing Michael and moving with Evan. I talked to Michael the next day, and he wouldn't answer me, only saying he couldn't take care of himself.

I moved around slowly as I went about my day figuring I had one more chance to talk some sense into Michael and Jackie. I knew they wouldn't talk to me on the phone, so I decided to show up unannounced at their condo to try to talk to them face to face.

Three weeks after 9/11, I mustered up the courage to go visit Michael and Jackie at their gated condominium in Los Angeles. I'd been there two times before after Evan was born, so I remembered where it was. The boys' dad had just picked them up for baseball practice, so I got in my car and headed for downtown L.A. The October sun was bright through the windows of my car and the air felt cool, yet warm.

When I drove up to the security gates I didn't think I could find a way to get in. I needed to be an invited guest. The thought went through my head that I should have been considered far more than a damn "invited guest." I wasn't thinking clearly about them living in a gated community and suddenly realized I probably wouldn't be able to visit unannounced. I drove up to the gate anyway.

"Your name please?" the security guard asked.

I gave him my name. He called them and knew they were going to turn me away.

"I'm sorry, but the residents do not wish to see you." My heart sank and my eyes closed. They were so predictable.

"Really? Can you please tell them that I need to see them even if they don't want to see me?" I swallowed hard knowing I was going to have to say why. "As you can see, I am very pregnant and I am a surrogate mother for them. Recently, they informed me they no longer want their babies."

His young face remained emotionless but his eyebrows went up with surprise.

"Please call them back and say that if they don't come down to see me, I will tell every person in this complex what is going on, and I will call the media."

"Yes, ma'am, I'll tell them." He grabbed the phone to deliver my message.

"Ms. Fletcher will be down to see you. Drive over to the parking lot on the side by the fountain and she will meet you there." He looked at my belly touching the steering wheel as I pulled forward.

"Thank you," I said. Ms. Fletcher, not Mrs? I thought. I was sure I would never call the media, but you can bet I might have called out to them from outside the window. I was desperate, and desperate people do desperate things.

The guard buzzed me through the gate and I drove over to the fountain and got out of my car. The foliage was beautiful, green, and colorful flowers were all around me. I smelled a hint of jasmine close by as I sat down by a brick planter full of red and white impatiens. I wondered how they could afford this condo. I waited for about ten minutes before I saw Jackie walking through the gate holding the baby. I knew her instantly by her stiff thin lips. She was wearing a thin white airy top with dark jeans and red lipstick. My mood softened when I saw Evan. I didn't think she would bring him. I melted at the sight of him and wondered if he was being taken care of. He looked okay, still wearing the helmet. She sat down without saying a word.

He'd grown so much since the last time I saw him. He would turn one later this month. As she sat, Evan reached his chubby little hand out to me. I raised mine back, and our fingers touched. He grabbed onto my finger. She handed him to me without hesitating.

"So, we already told you what to do, Susan, why all the drama?"

"Me, drama? Seriously? I didn't come to argue, Jackie."

"Well then, do what you are told and put them into foster care or social services, or whatever. Michael will get them when he can, but it might be a few years. I'm moving at the end of the month back to Boston with Evan and I've divorced Michael."

"That's it? You think it's that easy? They are all full siblings, Jackie."

"Don't you think I'm aware of that fact?" She pushed her shoulder-length black hair back.

Evan bounced joyfully in what was left of my lap. I pulled him to my side and held him with one arm while he stood on the bench. He was a happy baby, but his helmet still worried me. Were they taking care of him the right way?

"I can't believe this is happening. Where is Michael?" I asked, hoping I could talk to someone more helpful than Jackie.

"He wouldn't come down. He's been depressed since 9/11 and everything that's happening. He's had sporadic mental breaks and his overall mental health is not good. He's gone off his meds due to many negative triggers, especially 9/11."

"What do you mean?" I asked as fear rose up inside me.

"9/11 triggered him into a downward spiral. His aggressive bipolar diagnosis keeps him agitated unless he takes meds. I used to be able to control him, but without the meds I cannot."

"I don't know what to say to you, Jackie. I'm almost speechless that you can be so heartless. You both started this and you both need to take responsibility."

"Michael lost a huge financial deal with his business, and his mother won't help him anymore. Believe it or not he is a genius, but it's masked by his bipolar diagnosis."

It felt like she was trying to persuade me to see it her way. It was insane.

"I'm gone as of the end of the month," she said again. "Michael and I are done. I can't live with him anymore. Do what you are supposed to do with the twins, and Michael will handle it from that point on. I do not want more babies, I'm done and I want out. End of conversation."

"End of conversation, huh? Ah no, I don't think so." I had no idea what to say except the blatant truth. "I will never, ever give the twins to social services, Jackie. Ever." I knew this to be true as sure as anything I have ever believed in.

She got up to leave and reached out for Evan.

I didn't want to hand him over, and when I did he started to whimper.

"I see your time is limited," she said full of pity as she pointed to my belly. "You can't fix everything." She shushed him and walked away.

It was the last time I would see my first surrogate baby. My heart hurt wondering if he was fully cared for, especially since they didn't want the twins. I thought about calling social services to share my concern for Evan, but I knew I had to let it go. That very same moment I wanted to scratch her eyes out for being so mean, and shook my head in wonder at how she could be so cold-hearted.

I stayed on the bench after she left wondering why I even wasted my time trying to make this work, but now I knew for sure she wanted nothing to do with the twins. She wanted Michael to take over but he couldn't. He couldn't take care of himself, let alone twins.

I continued my search for legal advice because I needed all the help I could get. After a few weeks and many unresponsive calls, Richard Walton called me back to tell me that he would represent me "under certain conditions."

"You are up against a lot here, Susan, and I understand your position," He said. "However, you must understand my point of view is to protect the parents' rights." He was firm, but he didn't believe they didn't want their babies. In my mind, they were not going to change their minds, but part of me still didn't believe it either.

"I thought about what you are up against alone, and if after the birth you need me, I'll be there for you," Richard said over the phone.

He told me he had talked to Lauren and Tracey to verify my story and felt sure that I wouldn't need his help. His last words were to all of us were, "The parents will come around. I know they will."

All I could think during and after our conversation was, what about *my* rights in this whole mess? What about *the babies'* rights? It was as if we didn't even matter. Both Lauren and Tracey were acting weird, and I couldn't find any help online. They didn't know what to do. Everyone was disengaged from any agreement we had, and I couldn't trust anyone. If it didn't work out with Richard, I could always represent myself, but I needed as much help as possible. I couldn't shake the thoughts and feelings of everything being totally unknown, and wondering what was next. The most important thing was that the twins had a mommy and daddy on the day they were born, but it didn't look like that was going to happen.

As I fought through the denial of it all, I felt no compassion for Michael and Jackie. It was time for me to take charge and I promised the twins that no matter what I would always be there for them, making it feel like they became mine at that very moment. I knew realistically they weren't, but I had to protect them and be there for them.

At a little over thirty-three weeks pregnant the birth order still wasn't done. The birth order request required Michael and Jackie to hire an attorney to draw up the paperwork to allow them to have their names name on the birth certificate, at the hospital, when the twins are born. Otherwise, they would not be listed on the birth certificate and I would automatically be listed as the mother, per the state of California. After what Jackie told me, I doubted a pre-birth order was going to happen.

At thirty-four weeks pregnant, I felt labor was imminent, but I couldn't judge when because I'd never been pregnant with twins. I was *huge*. My belly button was ripe and flat and my skin stretched so much that it was hard as marble. My due date was in early December, but I knew I would not make it that far. With a typical twin pregnancy it's known that they come earlier than a single birth, sometimes by four weeks. So instead of forty weeks, they are expected at thirty-six weeks gestation.

I carried them low and could feel the pulsing of my waters just above my pubic bone. I knew the twin on the bottom was bigger than the one on the top. I lifted them up often with my hands and sat down whenever I could. A short catnap consumed me every mid-day; I slept the minute I placed my head anywhere—the couch, the floor, the car, it didn't matter where I was, slumber would come to re-energize me.

I fell asleep at a stoplight while thinking about Brian at sixth grade science camp, away from home for the first time. I awoke abruptly when my car inched forward slowly as my foot came off the brake. Before I knew it, my car was in a busy intersection with horns blaring and cars coming to an abrupt stop to avoid hitting my car. I smelled the odor of burnt rubber through the window. I looked at the clock and saw it was 1:30 p.m. I pulled my head up to see one last car screeching to a stop a foot away from my door. Blurred faces yelled and screamed at me while I pulled to the side of the road trembling to catch my breath, my humongous belly just under the wheel.

I got home that afternoon and dropped my compact on the floor in the bathroom. I looked over at Boomer guarding the door like a good boy. It was the first time I actually wondered if I should bend over and pick up what I dropped. I looked into the mirror and decided to leave it on the floor after seeing the size of my belly, and then got in bed.

The next day I told Lauren and Tracey about what happened with my car and wanting to sleep all the time. I was sure it was just compounded stress because Brian was away for the week.

A few days later, they had a psychologist call me. "Do you want to talk?" she asked.

I assured her I was fine, just tired plus there was no way in hell I was going to talk to her about what was really going on. What could she possibly tell me? I was sure she hadn't gone through something like this, and I knew she was Tracey's and Lauren's friend and anything I said would get back to them one way or another, so I declined. Instead, I talked my heart out to Adam, who was a good listener. I confided in Terrie, too, and filled them both in on everything. They were just as stunned as everyone else.

No one had any answers or knew what to do.

18

Understanding the Unbelievable

Brian's birthday was this week, and it was time to pick him up from sixth grade science camp. Steven and I missed him like crazy. After we celebrated Brian's birthday that night, Brian, Steven, and I were getting ready to watch a movie after dinner. The twins were kicking nonstop on both sides of my abdomen. When they both kicked at the same time my belly literally danced all around the top, bottom, and the sides. The boys sat in amazement watching life move and kick inside me, laughing and giggling so hard it made Boomer bark thinking it was a game. They'd push my belly in and one of the twins would kick back.

I had tried to keep what was going on with Michael and Jackie away from Brian and Steven, but I had no idea what I was protecting them from. They overheard me on the phone from time to time or heard Theresa and I talking late at night. One of them would poke his head up from downstairs and come to me for a motherly snuggle.

Because I was so far along and without hearing from Michael and Jackie, I realized it was time to tell the boys that the twins might be coming home with us. I didn't want them to be surprised, but I had no idea what I was going to say. I turned the volume down before the movie started.

"So, I think you guys know we are having some problems with Michael and Jackie, right?"

They both looked at me with worried faces.

"Kinda," Brian said.

"Well, you're right. Bri. We are and the problem is pretty serious." Both faces studied me with genuine concern.

"I don't know how to say this except to just tell you the truth. Michael and Jackie don't want the twins, their babies that are in my tummy." I laid my hand on my large bump and their eyes followed.

"Why?" Steven asked.

"Well, it's complicated, honey, but Jackie changed her mind and Michael has an illness that we didn't know about and he can't take care of himself."

"What are you going to do, Mom?" Brian asked.

"I wanted to tell you both because there might be chance that Mommy will bring the twins home after they are born." My lip started to quiver and my heart ached.

"Okay, Mom," Brian said. "We'll help you. Will they stay with us forever and be like our brother and sister?"

"Well, no. That's the complicated part. They are not your brother and sister. They would be with us for a short time until I can find them a mommy and daddy to love them."

"Okay, Mommy," Steven said. "I would like a sister or a brother to play with."

"Maybe in the future, honey, but not now." I felt myself starting to fall apart, but I couldn't break now. They needed me. "It's real important to Mommy that you know they are not your brother and sister, okay?"

"Okay," they both said.

"Just remember you can ask Mommy anything, okay? If you have questions later, let me know. I'll answer any questions you have, no matter what they are."

The next day I got a call from Mrs. Robinson, Steven's teacher. She asked me to meet her after school that day and told me that it was important. I was worried something was wrong, but she said everything was okay she just had some questions. I figured it might have something to do with his homework.

I went to the school fifteen minutes before it let out and showed up at the front door of the classroom. She waved me over to the back of the room while the children worked. Steven peeked up at me, smiled, and put his head back down, diligently working on his project. I made my way to the back of the room.

"So, you are pregnant," she whispered.

I looked at her bewildered.

"Steven shared with me today that you are having twins for someone else, but now they changed their minds and you are bringing them home with you." Her voice went up five octaves on the last three words.

"Yes, what Steven said is true," I said, worried it might get out. The less I said, the better.

"It was funny because I asked him if you were pregnant and if the twins were his brother and sister and he was adamant that they are not your babies or his brother or sister."

"That is true, they are not ours. I am a surrogate mother."

"*Oh*," she said, exaggerating the *Oh*. "That makes sense now." She laughed softly.

I realized that I would have to tell her the story, or at the very least the short version, because of my present situation. She may see me with the twins later, I thought.

"I agreed to be a surrogate mother again for the same couple I delivered a son for just a year ago. They have some issues and are backing out of our surrogacy agreement," I said it without emotion. It gave me a sense of security to leave the emotion out with people I didn't know well.

"What? How can that happen?" she said, her mouth remaining open in surprise.

I looked at Mrs. Robinson, who had just married her

childhood sweetheart earlier that summer. She couldn't have been more than twenty-something. Steven loved her and talked about her all the time. She was so good with her class and put passion into her work with the kids. She drew little hearts on Steven's homework and on everything she did. Her golden hair swept over one eye with bangs, and her blue-green eyes stared at me like she had a burning question to ask.

"My husband and I have been trying to get pregnant now since two years before we got married and have had no luck. I'm shocked that these people could do this to their own children. And you had another one for them? I'm speechless."

"I know, it's hard for me to believe too, but it's true." I wanted to try to make a quick getaway because I couldn't believe the number of people I ran into that were experiencing infertility problems and felt completely open to talk about it with me. The school alarm rang signaling the end of the day.

"Could you please keep this quiet so others don't find out? I just want to make sure the twins are taken care of first."

"Sure, of course. I just wanted to make sure everything was okay at home."

I smiled. "Thank you," I said and turned to go. She gazed longingly at my huge pregnant bump.

That very moment, I wished so hard that I could help her instead of Michael and Jackie.

A few nights later, the boys helped me with the grocery shopping as they often did. After we piled groceries into the cart, I went to find an open check stand in the front of the store. I couldn't wait to get home and put my feet up.

A checker named Alice was behind the register with no one in her line, and she was smiling at us as we made our way to her line. She was a fixture at this store. She was probably a little older than me and had long black hair down to her waist, braided in ponytails with strands of gray. She was always happy and often said she loved being a cashier because she learned a lot about her regular customers with her endless questions. The boys stared at her long purple nails with colorful tiny flowers painted on them.

"Hi you guys. How are you all?" she asked. "Oh! Look at Mom! It looks like you are going to have a new brother or sister soon."

"It's twins," Steven exclaimed brightly.

"Oh wow, how cool is that? Maybe you will get two sisters and even up the score?"

"No, Mom said they are not ours," Steven said. "Even though the parents don't want them."

Uh oh, I thought. Here we go again. I wanted them to tell the truth and be proud, but this wasn't the time. My tummy was sticking out for the world to see and most people didn't hesitate to comment about it.

Alice's face turned from happy to suddenly serious. She looked at me. "What?"

Steven turned his head up to look at me. I smiled at him and looked back at Alice as I watched Brian load the groceries into the cart.

"I'm a surrogate mother carrying twins for another couple," I said casually, hoping she didn't hear all of what Steven said. I inched my way over to the cart and paid for our groceries.

"Oh, I didn't know that. How wonderful. I've never met one of those before."

One of those? I thought.

"Um, I mean a surrogate," she corrected herself, likely feeling embarrassed, and then she wished us well as we left the store.

Sometimes ignorance is bliss.

Very early the next morning, I began having hard, shooting labor pains. It was a few days past my thirty-fourth week and I knew I had to try to keep the babies in as long as possible. I lifted my heavy tummy and walked with my arms supporting my belly and got the boys off to school.

Later, I checked my computer and saw two emails from Adam with a subject line "Call me." I hesitated because the emails were over the span of the last few days. I didn't have time to call him right now, though. I pulled myself up from what I thought was a strong contraction. I responded to one of the emails and typed, "I'm going into labor. I'll call you when I can."

I grabbed my bag and called Tracey and Lauren to let them know I was in early labor. I was feeling low-level contractions with a few major ones and they were getting closer and closer. I went back to my computer to add to another email to Adam. "It looks like I will be bringing the twins home with me, too. S."

Lauren and Tracey responded by showing up in front of my house in the car together. I rolled my eyes at both of them wanting to come with me because I was sure they enjoyed Dr. Kazman's company more than mine. Dr. Kazman told them to bring me to his office first, before the hospital. They both dressed perfectly when we went to see him and always brought him homemade treats. It was great to have some extra help and a driver, though.

When we got to Dr. Kazman's office, I felt a rush of euphoria. I was there, but not there. It was a surreal feeling.

"Hop up here, Suz, let's take a look," Dr. Kazman said patting the exam table. He was the one who told me, "No matter what happens, know you are doing the right thing. It will all work out."

He always made me feel comfortable. His office across the hall had pictures of his two little girls all over the wall, and I could tell what a wonderful daddy he was. The last time I was at his office he told me, "You're an amazing, happy pregnant woman, so textbook. I wish more of my patients were like you." I rarely whined about stuff, because I did love being pregnant.

"How are you feeling?"

"Not that great, I feel really heavy and I'm worried about

well, everything." I felt overwhelmed with my life. He looked concerned because I was never that grim. "Something is wrong," I whined.

"Okay, let's take a look." He pushed his round rim glasses up on top of his nose and took his stethoscope into his hands and put it on my heart.

After examining me, he said Lauren and Tracey, "We need to get her over to L&D at the hospital to be checked for leakage of amniotic fluid and schedule a full Level II scan to see how the babies are doing."

I got up and waddled to the door.

19

Pre Labor Shock

On a dreary early morning in November, two short months after 9/11, the whole world felt like it was still in disarray. It wound up being a long day in the hospital and I was sick with worry about my own kids while I was stuck there. Lauren and Tracey promised they'd take care of the boys and make sure they got fed, and went to school the next day.

I landed in one of the largest hospitals in Los Angeles with no rooms available. Dr. Kazman found a large closet and wheeled my bed into it himself with the brooms and buckets against in the corner. The nurses followed him, moving all the supplies out of the way to fit my bed inside. Dr. Kazman calmed me with drugs and determined after tests that my amniotic fluid was in fact leaking a very small amount. The twins were fine, but I was told to take it easy and rest. This was the hospital bed rest I was trying to avoid, but I knew I had to keep the twins in my womb as long as possible because every day mattered.

The beeping of the new IV/Blood Pressure machines was annoying, especially with the little yellow light blinking off and on, but the white noise from the air conditioning calmed me. Late that evening, I surrendered to a deep resting peace. I felt myself drift in and out of sleep until I heard what I thought was a harsh whisper say, *"Run away with me, Susan. We'll build a world together with the twins, and your children. We can be a family together."*

I'm not sure those were the exact words, but it was pretty close. My eyes popped open and I saw the shadow of a large man behind the tiny light of my IV machine.

I squinted to see who it was, but it was too dark in the closet. I didn't recognize the voice, but I heard the low, deep tone of a man's voice. Was I dreaming?

I closed my eyes again thinking that I needed to settle my mind. I'd been given a sedative to calm my body, so I was loopy and I could feel the dizziness. I started to drift off to sleep again.

I heard the door open and I opened my eyes. I saw light from outside and heard someone shuffling toward me.

I saw half of Michael's face in front of me with a tender look in his eyes. Michael, the intended father to the twins. What the hell was he doing here and how did he know I was here? I didn't have time to call anyone before I left the house, and I wasn't sure if Lauren or Tracey called him. Where was Jackie? I didn't know what to say after everything that had happened, but I was scared beyond belief. I thought I heard what he said and wanted to confirm that I wasn't imagining it.

"What?"

"We can make a family together," he said.

The drugs in my system seemed to wear off immediately, and I was jolted back to reality. Fear coursed through my veins. My first thought was to grab the hospital call monitor for help, but there wasn't one. I was in a closet. My biggest fear was crazy people, and it seemed I'd chosen one to carry babies for. He loomed over my humongous belly, making me feel incredibly vulnerable. Even death didn't scare me as much as crazy people because you can't predict what they are going to do and then they say crazy shit, like he just did.

I didn't want to enrage him, but I wanted to get far, far away from him, and keep my belly safe. Steven and Brian popped into my mind. I needed to protect them, but I couldn't because I was here in bed under doctor's orders to stay put. I couldn't walk without leaking amniotic fluid. I had to stay in bed to keep the twins safe. The boys were sleeping at home with Terrie looking after them. I needed to call her to warn her.

I moved my hands over the top of my belly, and said, "What did you just say?" I still didn't believe a word of it. His dark black hair fell over his eyes and he was unshaven and looked uneasy.

"I know I could get my family trust again if I showed my mother I'm responsible."

I knew getting him upset would solve nothing, so I chose my words carefully.

"Oh, that sounds interesting, yeah um, all of it, but, um, why are you here?"

He moved closer to me.

I held my breath.

"Jackie called to tell me you were in labor and a nurse friend of hers called to let her know that you had checked into the hospital with labor pains," he explained. "I thought about our situation a lot, and I think you and I might have a chance together, being that you are single and all. What do you think? I mean, we both love kids, and this way we could stay together and we wouldn't have to give up the twins. They are mine you know, my babies, and Jackie could keep Evan like she wants to do."

I was terrified at his suggestion. Of course I knew they were his babies, but I also knew he couldn't take care of them, and I didn't want to be a part of anything he was dreaming up.

"I thought you and Jackie didn't want the twins. You told me that, and the agency said you couldn't handle any of it. You breached our contract, Michael. How am I supposed to believe anything you say?"

I didn't want to argue because I didn't know if he was melting down, and I didn't know anything about bipolar disorder. For all I knew, he could pull out a knife and it'd all be over. It was still dark in the room. All I could see was part of his face. I noticed his hands were behind his back, which made me extremely fearful.

"Why does everyone keep saying that?" he said sternly.

I had to get out of this conversation because I felt so exposed. I inched my way up to a sitting position like I was interested in what he was saying. In truth, I was caught in something I didn't know how to get out of.

He kept talking. "I have this new idea and you are in it with your kids of course. We can do this because the twins are almost here. We can go away and do our own thing, be a family like in another country."

My mind was grabbing for any part of reality to figure out what to do, and my survival instincts kicked in. I made it to a sitting position and grabbed my tummy as if I was in sheer pain.

"Oh, oh my God, my stomach hurts," I groaned. I grabbed it screaming like the terrible actor I was. Startled, he moved away from my bed toward the door with a surprised look and opened the door all the way until I could see him clearly.

"Oh, God. I feel awful. It hurts. Please call the nurse!"

He ran out of the room, and a nurse hurried in a few moments later.

"What's the matter? Where is the pain?" She turned me over to my left side and moved closer to me to feel and touch everywhere.

"Here, and here," I said pointing to my stomach. Michael was near the door but far enough away that I could whisper to the nurse, "Please get him out of here and shut the door." I trembled with fear and felt ice cold.

She turned around and looked at him. "I have to do an exam, please leave," she said and ushered him out the door, shutting it behind him.

"What the hell is going on here?" the surprised nurse asked. "Who let him in here?"

"We did. He's the father right?"

"Yes, he's the father, but he is the intended father to me. I'm the surrogate mother and he is not my husband. It's a long story, and we have a very strained relationship right now. I don't want him anywhere near me, or the twins. I'm afraid of him." I was hyperventilating.

The nurse looked at me puzzled.

"Look, his wife told me a few months ago that he has bipolar disorder and he is off his meds." She looked at me like I was the crazy one. I had to say more so she would believe me.

"I didn't know this until a few days before 9/11. He also breached our surrogate contract and told my agency he has no interest in the twins. I'm not lying. Ask Dr. Kazman, he'll tell you."

She moved toward the broom closet door, analyzing me to see if what I was saying was true.

"Now he's here while I am in early labor asking me to run away with him." A flurry of thoughts went through my head. I had no idea he had any kind of feelings for me, but I definitely didn't have any feelings for him. Zero. "I think it has something to do with his mental state with how he is acting," I added.

Her forehead wrinkled upward and she headed out the door, closing it behind her.

I thought about the birth of Evan a year before when Michael was between my legs watching his son being born. I cringed, now thinking what a stupid idea it was to let him see Evan being born, but Jackie had been there too, so I felt like it was okay.

I realized that my life looked like a crazy drama-filled TV reality show, or a soap opera.

The nurse came back in.

"You can call my doctor or my attorney," I told her. "They will verify my story, and give you the information you need."

"I called hospital security. They'll be here as soon as possible."

Two burly men with balding heads came into my room within minutes wearing heavy khaki colored jackets. After 9/11, there was zero tolerance for security issues in the hospitals. One held a nightstick and a large flashlight.

How did I get myself into this? I felt my body shaking.

The nurse said to the men, "The man outside this door needs to be escorted out of this hospital. He is not welcome here."

"Yes, ma'am," they said in unison and went outside the door where Michael was waiting.

"Your visit is over sir," I heard one of them say.

"But I haven't finished talking to Susan. We need to talk about our future," he said. The nurse looked at me with validation.

"She doesn't want to talk to you right now. You can call her later," one guard with a deep voice offered.

The other said in a low voice, "Now please, follow us, sir. You will be leaving the hospital, and do not come onto the premises again or we will be forced to call the police and have you arrested."

It freaked me out thinking how insane it would be to call the police on the intended father. One guard moved slowly to the left of Michael and one went to the right, staying closely alongside him to escort him out. He didn't fight.

The door was still open. Michael looked at me over his shoulder. "Why are you doing this? Can't we talk?"

I didn't want to talk to him if he was talking like this. I had to protect the babies, my own kids, and myself. I couldn't trust him or ever let him in my home again. Crazy people did crazy things and I'd never seen him like this before. He had a desperate look in his eyes that chilled me as if he had been stalking me the whole time. I thought about my kids again, knowing I would have to call Terrie to give her a heads-up in case Michael showed up at the house. I thought of what that conversation might be like. "Oh, by the way, Terrie, Michael might show up at the door. Don't open it and call 9-1-1."

I regretted choosing them as intended parents.

Why didn't they ask him to see a psychologist in the screening process like I had to go through as a surrogate? Doubt entered my mind over my own intuition. Was I making too much of this?

A strong voice came from within. "Oh hell no," I said softly. These same questions kept going through my mind and my feelings grew stronger that it was important to follow my instincts to be safe. It's what I knew best, or what I thought I knew best. I asked the nurse for a phone to call the agency.

Lauren and Tracey had just been at the hospital with me and had left about 11 p.m. that evening. I looked over at wall clock and saw that it was now 2:45 a.m. A few short hours ago, Lauren told me to call her beeper if there was anything I needed. I beeped her and she called me back quickly. I started to feel pain again and sobbed.

"What's going on, Susan? Are you okay?"

"No, I'm not okay. I need your help. Michael showed up here at the hospital. Did you or Tracey call him?"

"What?" she nearly screamed. "No, no we didn't, there was no time. Is everything okay, are you in labor?"

"No, well at least I don't think so, but I can't get up unless I have to go to the bathroom, and I'm a wreck. Michael asked me to run away with him."

"What?" she exclaimed.

"Yeah, I'm serious. Jackie was right. He's off his meds and acting weird. I don't know what to do."

"We'll be right there."

"Wait, let Terrie know just in case he goes to the house. I want her to know *not* to let him in if he goes to the door. The boys need to be with someone at all times. I'm serious, Lauren. I'm not messing around. This is important."

"Okay, we'll do that. Is this even possible? How can this be fucking happening?"

"Lauren, this is something I would not screw with you on. I am dead serious."

"I know, I know. I just can't fucking believe this shit. I'm calling Tracey now. Goodbye."

Less than an hour later, Lauren and Tracey laid down to sleep on a roll-away mattress in the corner of a hospital room the nurses found for me. I watched them hold and straighten their perfect hair before they hit the hard cushion so it would stay in place if they somehow they managed not to move while they slept.

The next morning was the day before Thanksgiving. Dr. Kazman left a strict protocol for me until my body settled down, as well as rules for the nurses not giving out information and about security in case Michael showed up again. My life was on hold as it had been since the day of the embryo transfer thirty-four weeks earlier.

I wondered what would have happened if I had stayed pregnant with triplets. I probably would have been in the hospital for an extended period of time with these drugs to prevent labor. I shuddered at the thought and swore I would never take those drugs again. I was so sick vomiting up my stomach lining over and over again. It started the moment Dr. Kazman started me on harsh drugs to stop labor until they were out of my system, leaving my ankles and knees swollen to triple their size as a result. Migraines took over my body, paralyzing me. I probably would have given birth early with triplets and I'm certain they would have ended up in the NICU. I can't imagine where I would have been financially with that scenario and began to be somewhat content with the decision I had made all those months ago, but wouldn't acknowledge it.

I went home two days after Thanksgiving walking with one foot in front of the other and moving things out of the way with my feet everywhere I went. I was so big and couldn't see the ground in front of me when I walked. I avoided sitting on the couch unless I was going to be there for a long time, because it meant I would have to get up again. It was an especially cool winter, but the twins provided warmth from their bodies to mine that I'd never felt before.

My hormone-soaked brain was in overdrive, my senses were heightened, and I could sense how people felt by watching their facial expressions and body language like an alert animal anticipating danger.

Michael and Jackie didn't return phone calls, and I felt like they had completely written us off as if we'd never happened. My daycare was proving difficult to maintain, and I don't remember how I took care of my kids let alone the kids from the daycare, but I did. I was so exhausted mentally and physically that I barely remember some of those days.

Our goal of thirty-six weeks gestation was a few days away, which was a normal time for twins to be born. I continued to have labor pains and when they were closer together and they didn't stop, I called Lauren and Tracey again.

"Come on, Susan, get up!" Tracey yelled as she tried to shove my pregnant ass into Lauren's high Suburban. By the time they showed up at my house, the labor pains were intense and my belly was as hard as a rock with a major contraction holding it hostage. I held onto the seat of the car by the sidewalk breathing out my contraction.

"Wait!" I screamed as it peaked over my body. They both hopped out to help push me into the car after the contraction. There was no way these two petite girls could get my big ass up and into the car, I thought. We did it, but I have no idea how.

I felt that imminent feeling of no going back now. Labor was coming, my intuition said. I was thirty-five weeks and five days pregnant and these babies were definitely ready to come out. However, after my checkup at the hospital with Dr. Kazman, he said, "Time to go home again, Susan."

He said it like he had said it hundreds of times. I was so tired. I headed to the hospital bathroom defeated, slowly walking and not wanting to leave after yet another false alarm. I couldn't believe my body was lying to me. It felt like labor, like it was time. My belly felt so low, like the twins were going to come out at any moment.

I got up from the toilet and reached down to grab my pants. Fluid came rushing out of me like a large wave all over the bathroom floor. I watched it spill and fan out under the bathroom door, where everyone waited for me. Some amniotic fluid pooled in the open hem of my leggings, leaving just enough for me to dip my finger in. I brought it up to my lips and tasted it—salty, like the ocean, and how I imagined it to taste. I wanted to make sure it wasn't just pee. It was time, they were ready, and so was their surrogate mother.

"Help," I said in a low tone. I was unable to move or bend over to get my pants. The intense labor pains hit unexpectedly, and I doubled over in pain. I found the help string in the bathroom and pulled it hard. It felt like a voice I didn't have.

Dr. Kazman rushed in with Lauren and Tracey, and they called a handful of nurses. He put his arms around me and guided me as I baby-stepped out of the bathroom with my black pants still between my ankles, everything soaked.

"Set up the delivery room, it's baby time," he shouted happily to the nurses.

PART THREE

20

Megan and Matthew's Birth

The twins were born on a Thursday in late November 2001. I, too, had been born on a Thursday. "Thursday's child has far to go," the old English nursery rhyme goes.

Dr. Kazman, Lauren, Tracey, six nurses, and eight interns were in the delivery room when the twins came into the world. Dr. Kazman masterfully conducted our delivery without a baton, using his hands like an orchestra conductor, swishing nurses to the left, singing to the interns on the right about what to do and not do. "Push," he said to me, and then looked over at the interns and said, "Wait," with his left arm in the air. Everyone stopped and looked at him. "Push and wait," he said, arms waving above his head. I howled and screamed at each peak contraction and just when I felt like giving up he said, "Breathe," in a whisper three inches from my face. His breath was heavenly and I felt like I could kiss him. He was the best birth coach I'd ever had. Hands down. He made sure the interns were watching along with Tracey and Lauren.

Baby Girl was born first. The nurses ushered her off to clean up and check her vitals. It felt like she was crying for me, with good healthy cries bouncing off the walls of the room. It felt so strange to bear down again for another, when one baby was already crying in the room. It was the amazing miracle of birthing twins.

After a few minutes of pushing, Dr. Kazman hopped up onto the bed, straddling me while physically using his body to usher out Baby Boy. He was pushing hard. "Come on, Susan, make me look good," he whispered as I let out my last breath and pushed hard and felt Baby Boy come out of my body. The room filled with the most beautiful music I could hear that day—two healthy newborns crying at the top of their lungs.

The nurse scooped him up and checked his vitals. I knowingly looked over at Lauren and Tracey and said, "This is it." The three of us knew what we would have to do if Michael and Jackie didn't show up, even though we didn't talk about it.

"They are perfect, Susan, just perfect," Lauren said. Tracey nodded. I felt so proud, yet so scared of what might happen. The minute I saw them there together crying out, my maternal instincts kicked up and I felt a tremendous responsibility to them. Happy tears that they were healthy filled my eyes.

They were born within 45 minutes of my water breaking and 7 minutes apart. They both weighed close to seven pounds each. Two nurses brought them to me one at a time. I reached out one arm and held one carefully, then the other and cuddled them, smelling their little newborn heads. Everyone made their way out of the room except Dr. Kazman, Lauren, and Tracey.

"Welcome to the world little ones," I said as I held them close and kept them warm.

They immediately went to the side looking for food and squeaked the whole way like newborns do. It looked like they were ready to eat. I decided not to breastfeed because I didn't want to get too close. It would be way too much bonding for me.

I closed my eyes and took a deep breath. I wasn't afraid to hold them, but so afraid to get too close.

I made a promise to find them a real mother and a father. Rarely did I make a promise I couldn't keep. It seemed necessary to promise them while I was pregnant to feel some sense of comfort and stability and it seemed easy enough to keep my promise because Michael and Jackie didn't want them, but my sensible side knew there might be problems later. No one knew what would happen and no one had any answers yet. There were no instruction manuals, no maps, and no how-to on where to go.

Nothing.

I handed the twins to Lauren and Tracey so Dr. Kazman could finish up with me. Lauren wanted the girl and Tracey wanted the boy. "This one is mine," Lauren said. Tracey said the same about Baby Boy. Dr. Kazman said everything with me physically looked fine, especially for a twin birth. I felt so relieved and grateful.

I pictured myself strolling the twins to the Supreme Court with my boys alongside me. I couldn't turn to anyone because even the handful of attorneys I talked to during the pregnancy didn't know what to do. I could only assume there would be legal and financial issues, but more important now, what do I do? Take the twins home? I knew my chances of fulfilling my promise to them was pretty slim because the law was in favor of protecting intended parents, especially after the whole Baby M case. My future promise seemed bleak, but I wasn't going to give up so easily.

A few hours later, Tracey and Lauren left for the night to get some sleep and they moved me into a postpartum room with the twins. I thought about the options given to me during the pregnancy and wondered what to do next. Per my semi-hired attorney, who did not believe the parents would do a no-show, I had three choices in the state of California:

1. Hand the twins over to social services.

2. Become a mother to the twins and co-parent with the father, Michael.

3. Go for parentage myself.

Number 1 and 2 were absolute no go's, so I had one choice

and I was struggling with it because I didn't know what would happen. If I took my case to court, I didn't know if I could win, especially because I was not the twins' biological mother.

There were questionable days ahead, but I couldn't get my mind off one thing. I'm bringing the twins home, but this was never supposed to happen. I thought about it over and over again, wanting an answer to why Michael and Jackie would do this.

I fidgeted and stared at the hospital door, willing it to open with the little bit of slim hope I had left to have Michael, Jackie, and Evan come through the door, ready to add to their family, but it wasn't going to happen. I listened to the doctor names being called on the overhead speakers and IV machines beeping down the hallway. My blue and white hospital gown had gotten twisted around me. Frustrated, I lifted it and pulled it around me to get untwisted. The hormones that made me feel so good during the pregnancy had plummeted after birth, and it felt like they were slowly draining from my body like the blood pouring out from between my legs. I felt like I'd been pushed off a steep cliff into oblivion. I squinted at the fogginess that came over my brain and tried to think straight. I wanted to be pregnant again. I laughed out loud at the thought while my eyes filled with tears. I had to get ahold of myself, even with that lost feeling.

The twins were nestled together beside me in a bassinet after they'd been fed. If only their mother could hear, see, and hold them. I couldn't get enough of their new baby smell from the top of their heads to the bottoms of their toes. Baby Girl had sweet, perfectly pursed red lips, and Baby Boy had long, beautiful eyelashes. They were the epitome of health and I was still caught up in the miracle of a twin birth. I counted their fingers and toes like any mother would and looked for other signs that they looked like Michael, only noting their dark hair and eyes.

I stared at them huddled together. What would Brian and

Steven think? How could I protect myself, and my children, along with taking care of the twins? An intense desire to protect them filled me, grabbing something deep inside and giving me strength I didn't know I had. I would fight for them no matter what.

I dozed off and woke up a few times throughout the night to feed and change them. Taking care of them all night proved difficult. When one cried, the other was sleeping. I couldn't get them both to sleep at the same time.

I was exhausted the next morning when a nurse came in to tell me that the hospital social worker would be coming in to see me. I'm sure she was coming to visit me to protect the hospital's interest. Everyone knew we were heading for court. The most important legal document, the pre-birth order, had not been completed by Michael or Jackie. The hospital was in the clear with California law because I was considered the natural mother, just having given birth to the twins. All we had was a signed contract by all parties breached early on by Michael and Jackie. The intent of the contract to create life lay as flat as the paper it was signed on.

When the matronly, gray-haired social worker opened the door to my room, I smelled burnt toast from the hallway lingering in the air like it did at home. I felt starved and tired. She sat down on my bed and put her arm on mine like a mother would to her daughter for a serious conversation. Her green eyes were warm and friendly and her gray hair was feathered back on both sides just past her ears. I don't remember her name.

"Honey, I know this is hard, but you have to make a choice." She lifted her hand to my shoulder. It felt a little pushy, like she had an agenda. I moved slightly away but didn't know what to say, and I was worried that if I said anything it might be used against me later on.

"You can take the twins home or send them to social services," she said. My heart pounded in my chest and my face felt hot and sweaty. She leaned in closer until her face was close to mine and looked at me like she didn't know what else to say. My mind went blank and I panicked feeling numb from a weird sense of fear when our eyes met, and we fell silent like mothers knowing this was a pivotal moment for the twins. An orderly came in with breakfast and I heard the clinking of trays outside my room, which snapped me out of it. I was so hungry.

"I know," I said when the orderly put the tray in front of me. "I've gone over it so many times in my mind. There is no way I can send them to social services. I just can't and won't do it." I lifted the lid off the main entrée and shoveled scrambled eggs into my mouth.

"Then you are going to keep them?" she said like it was the worst possible thing I could do. I put my fork down, annoyed. This conversation was heading somewhere I didn't want to go.

"I promised them I am going to find them a home and a real mother and father." I pushed my aching postpartum body back up against the head of the bed and felt the blood drench the heavy diaper between my legs.

"You're a single mother with two young children at home to think of," she said, almost begging. The corners of her eyes wrinkled up when she looked at me. "They'll find a wonderful home for them. You've done a magnificent job giving birth to them." She sounded condescending. I kept eating.

She pushed her palm into the bare skin of my forearm and nudged me. "You must know it's next to impossible for the courts to grant you parentage as a single mother, especially to twins, because they'll need more care."

Here it was, the conversation I didn't want to have.

Screw you lady, I thought, but instead I said, "Maybe, but it's the only thing we've got. I'll take it to the courts to decide. I already have an attorney, kind of. I'm going for full parentage."

She said nothing.

I glanced over at the twins, who were content and slept soundly together, their eyes shut tight as if nothing in the world were amiss. I wished they would sleep like that at night. It felt like we were a team of three, plus my own two kids, Terrie, our two big dogs, and my daycare kids, which equaled an even dozen in a small homey house in a quiet, well-to-do suburb of Los Angeles.

She got up from my bed, saying, "Okaaaay," in a sing-songy kind of voice and then rolled her eyes. It made me angry. As she moved toward the door, I smelled the classic perfume Jean Nate full of floral and musk. A warm memory of my sweet grandmother came to mind. She would have never in a million years imagined the miraculous science that created the situation I found myself in, nor would she have imagined the heartache.

"I'll bring in the birth certificates," she said and then headed out the door.

"Wait, what?" I whispered. I didn't realize, or somehow managed to forget that I might have to name them. I had no names picked out because I seriously hoped Michael and Jackie would show up, a hope I never let go of until that moment. She paused at the door.

"Okay, no never mind," I said. "Please bring the paperwork in, thank you."

This made it real for me.

When she brought the birth certificates back in, she handed them to me without a word. I sat alone while the twins slept, filling them out. Okay, so this is awkward, I thought. It felt like it did when I filled out birth certificates for my own boys, but different. I was the twins' mother in my heart, but my head fought it because I started this journey to help someone else have a child. I decided to give them my maiden last name and come up with first names. What else could I do except come up with names as if they were my own children? My potential attorney told me to leave their names as "A" and "B," but I voted that idea down. A and B, really?

The form asked for a mother, my mind stopped spinning. I hesitated, and then wrote my first name with my maiden last name. I had to use my maiden name because when my ex-husband found out I was doing surrogacy, he made sure I knew one thing. "I don't want anything to do with your surrogacy mess, and I don't want my last name on anything." I was never going to use his complicated last name anyway.

Next, I had to list a father. Who would that be? I didn't really know. I thought it might help later if my name only was on it, so I printed "unknown." I'd already been through one divorce and I certainly did not want to parent with Michael. I went back to the open lines on the birth certificates. What would be a good name for a boy, for a girl? Baby Boy started to cry. I picked him up and then Baby Girl started crying. Names are important, I thought. I decided to give it more thought and put the forms on the nightstand thinking about the importance of a name given at birth.

My given last name at birth was Ring. It was my biological father's last name given to him by his single, unmarried mother. She was a triplet with two other sisters and she died when my father was seven. He grew up a rebel living with one Ring family member for awhile, then moving to the next, never quite fitting into the Ring family. He never knew his biological father with another last name, but we did find out he was some big shot attorney in Chicago who had a fling with my grandmother while he was going to Stanford when she lived in Palo Alto, California. No one ever met him, and I don't even know if he ever knew he had a son, my father. Someone in the family said he knew and refused to acknowledge my father.

My father then abandoned our family, my mother, older brother, and sister and me just after I was born. I didn't know what he looked like and wouldn't meet him again until I was nineteen. My sister found him through the Dear Abby ads in the newspaper with his military records. By that time I'd built up a lot of resentment about him being an absent father especially because I'd had some pretty miserable stepfathers.

My mother was right when she said to us kids, "Be careful, he will end up breaking your heart."

She was right. The ultimate betrayal by my father came when the FBI showed up at my home looking for him for tax fraud. I kept my last name anyway, but only because of my strong-willed grandmother.

So far, men were not to be trusted in my world.

Back in the hospital, I kept the father listed as unknown on the birth certificate. I sat back in bed feeling justified by my actions, thinking that if Michael wanted to be on the birth certificate and if he really wanted to be a father, *then he'd better start acting like one.*

By mid-afternoon I was still thinking about birth certificates, names and reminiscing about old times. I was also learning how to expertly hold two babies at the same time. One of the nurses called it the "football hold." I had one baby in my arm and bent over the bassinet to scoop the other then softly bouncing them up and down to soothe their cries. When I stood, the inside of my legs ached with post-labor pains and my breasts pulsated with a tingling ache because my milk was coming in. They were hungry and I was tired, and they were going through formula so fast I swear they grew overnight. I buzzed the nurse for more formula and changed them. This was hard work, and we weren't even out of the hospital yet.

After the nurse came in to take the twins for a final screening of their newborn testing, I heard Tracey's fashionista boots clicking down the hospital hallway toward my room. She came around the curtain, swinging it to the side and plopped down into the chair beside me, letting out a big sigh.

"No answer, Susan. I tried again and again. Michael and Jackie are not answering my calls. I can't believe they didn't at least call to see how the twins were, you know? Assholes." She flipped her hair back between her fingers.

"Yeah I know, Tracey, I know." I didn't have anything new to say.

I glanced over at the birth certificates wondering if I should get her input on names, but dismissed the thought when I saw her perched in front of the mirror reapplying lipstick.

I grabbed the birth certificates and sat on the edge of the bed. I tried to choose my words wisely.

"I'm taking them home with me, Tracey."

She put down her lipstick and stared at me.

"What?" She sat back down in the chair. "Oh, Susan, I'm not sure that's what you should do. We should wait until we hear from your attorney. Lauren should have talked to him by now. We're not sure about this. You might want to keep them as your own if you do that."

"I don't care what anyone says. They are not going to social services and I never said anything about keeping them, Tracey. Someone has to stand up for them," I said. I looked back at her and for once she didn't say anything.

Lauren pulled the curtain by the door back and said, "I'm back."

Tracey bounced up from her chair, her arms shooting straight in the air. "We're taking the babies home with us," she said excitedly.

Lauren didn't flinch. She simply looked over at me like a mother hen. "No worries, we've got it covered." She waved car seat instructions up in the air. "Tracey, I need your help downstairs so we can put the car seats into the car. I stopped at Babies "R" Us and picked up two on the way back to the hospital. I haven't done this for like thirteen years. These new car seats are so fucking complicated."

"Hold on," I said. "How'd you know we would need the car seats? You told me not to buy anything."

"Now it's time, Susan. I know you and I know the so-called parents are not coming. I talked to your attorney, who is now your official attorney."

"What'd he say?"

"He couldn't believe they haven't answered. He said he was going to call you about the birth certificates and that we cannot make any health decisions for the twins, and if we have to name them, use Baby A and Baby B so the parents can name them later."

"I am not going to name them that, it's a ridiculous idea."

"Susan, they aren't yours to name," Tracey said.

"I know, but they won't be named A and B."

"Well, we gotta go," Lauren said in her motherly tone. "It's not a huge deal, Susan, just name them what you want and we can always change it later. Come on, Tracey, there is a lot to do. Let's get moving so we can take Susan and the twins home." She picked up her black leather Prada bag, grabbed Tracey's hand, and headed for the door.

On her way out she yelled, "Don't worry about the boys, we're taking care of them with Terrie. They want to talk to you when they get home from school, so you can call them at this number."

She raced back to my bedside and wrote down her home phone number on a small piece of paper. She was always in a hurry, but I was relieved. I missed my boys, and rarely spent a night without them. They knew Lauren and Tracey, and Brian knew Lauren's daughter, Jennifer. They went to the same school and were in the same grade.

"Where are the twins now?" she yelled from the hallway.

"At their last newborn check," I yelled, but didn't hear an answer reply, just the sound of Tracey's boots fading down the hallway.

I wondered what might be going through my boys' minds. I remembered telling them in the beginning that I was doing this for Michael and Jackie to help them with their family and never intended to bring babies home. Our first journey went smoothly and the boys got to see Evan right after he was born while I was in the hospital. We visited them with my mother a few months later at their condo. I was happy I took the time to talk to the boys about what might happen this time. We still didn't know if Michael and Jackie might change their minds again.

In all the excitement before I left for the hospital to have the twins, Brian came up to me as I was going out the front door and demanded an answer to the most important question; "Why don't they want their babies, Mom?" My little boy was growing up so fast right before my eyes.

I didn't know why, but it was important to answer his question so I said, "Sometimes adults do crazy, stupid things and I'm sure they have problems that we don't know about." I brought him up to me close and gave him my most loving hug.

"That's dumb," he said as I hugged him.

"I agree, Bri, but there are some things in life we don't have control over." I felt ridiculous making excuses for them and he knew it.

I didn't have a definitive answer and told him the only thing I knew. I'm bringing the twins home with me and we would take things day by day.

∞

21

Names and Birth Certificates

After dinner I sat up in my hospital bed. I thought about names for the twins sleeping soundly beside me. I needed two before we left in the morning, which seemed like one of the hardest things to do. Names are a part of who you are. It's something you carry throughout your life. I imagined what they would look like when they were grown and what they might enjoy doing. Would they go to college? What would they be? I thought about anything and everything and wondered if their new family would rename them. I hoped they wouldn't, but it was most likely they would. I had to go for full parentage myself, to be able to fully and legally adopt them out to a new family who would ultimately decide their final names.

"Okay you two, I need names for you because I will not use Baby A and Baby B like our attorney said to." After I concentrated on what I would name them if they were mine, the names came quickly. I thought about naming a girl. I might have more names for girls but the top one I had always loved was Megan. Then I added my middle name, Ann. Megan Ann Ring.

Boy names? Matthew Ryan. Matthew Ryan Ring. I picked up the paperwork and started to fill out the birth certificate, hesitating again when I got to the box for father of child, so I moved on to the next line. Mother of child. I'd already written my name. I left father of child as "unknown" and justified it by saying that I did not truly know if he was the father or not due to IVF, and I didn't have his date of birth or what state he was born in.

I called the nurses station to get supplies for the twins and a young nurse came in who helped pack me up with baby supplies for a few weeks. "You're going to need all you can get," she said. "Two are a handful."

They knew I had nothing at home, and I would have to go shopping to get other baby supplies when I got home, everything in twos.

I saw Dr. Kazman after he knocked softly at the door. The nurse smiled at him and she left.

"How ya doing, Susan?"

"Oh, okay," I said. "I'm just trying to think of what I'll need when I get home."

"The twins had great checkups, healthy and no issues at all," he said and sat on the edge of my bed.

"That's great." I looked over at them as they squeaked away and the reality of the situation slammed my mind like a freight train. A little voice inside said, "Don't get too close. Keep your distance."

Matthew started to cry. I picked him up and cuddled him to my breast and sat back while his sister slept like a little angel.

I felt like a new mother because the babies were with me.

"How do I separate myself from this, Dr. Kazman?" I asked. "Or should I try to at all? Do I need to keep a safe distance? What exactly do I need to do?" I rocked Matthew back and forth and glanced over at the birth certificates on the nightstand. "I just named them."

He looked over at the paperwork and shook his head, bewildered. After a bit of silence, he said, "I'm sorry you have to go through this, Susan, but I know so many women who would love to be in your position."

I nodded and said nothing because I felt like l was going to cry. For a girl who doesn't cry much, I was sure doing a lot of it. I regained my composure and said, "I want to ask you something about the delivery."

"What is it?"

"Did you get all of it during or after the labor?" I looked at Matthew with his eyes tightly shut in my arms.

"All of what?"

"Well, you know, the third baby? Did you see anything and were you able to get all of the tissue when you took out the placentas from the twins?" I felt awful for asking, but I had to know, and my question reflected my awkwardness.

He hesitated like he didn't know what I was talking about.

"I often saw a round ball of tissue in the ultrasounds with the twins," I said. Maybe he'd already forgotten.

He looked up at me, and I could see from his face that he finally understood and remembered. He cleared his throat and looked straight into my eyes. "Yes, I think we did get it all. I couldn't be one-hundred percent sure because I didn't see anything like that during the delivery or afterward, but I'm sure you'll be fine."

There was a long pause and he went on, "Also, the reduction done by Dr. Taylor was early enough in the pregnancy that much of the residue was probably absorbed back into your body," he said with fatherly concern. "You are going to be facing a lot of unchartered territory here, Susan. Keep calm and remember who you are."

"I will, I hope." Who was I anyway? A woman with two young kids of her own who tried to help another couple have a bigger family. Now I was taking them home? "How could they do this, Dr. Kazman? Why?" I asked, hoping for an answer, any answer.

"I don't know, Susan, I just don't know." He laid his hand on top of mine and rose up from the end of my bed. "I've got rounds to do, but I'll be back later, okay?"

"Okay, see you later." I put Matthew back down next to his sister.

I started to see my future flash before my eyes with two babies in tow. Dating would probably be non-existent. I wouldn't have any time to see Adam and my freedom would virtually be gone for a long while. I imagined the twins growing up with the boys, but it didn't fit. I didn't want to be a single mom to four. I had prepared myself to be the surrogate, not the mother.

After Dr. Kazman left I fell asleep, but that night the twins were up every hour. I didn't know which one to get first, and still felt sore from the birth, which made moving around difficult. A young, friendly, green-eyed nurse with red curly hair came in; she must have heard the crying.

"Looks like they are hungry," she said with an Irish accent. "Here you take Baby A, and I'll take Baby B." She opened the small bottles of ready-made formula.

"Okay, thanks."

"How does it feel to be a new mama to twins?"

Clearly, she hadn't gotten the memo or heard the gossip around the hospital.

"Are you going to breastfeed?" she asked sweetly. "I can show you how."

"Well, no," I said. "But thank you."

I didn't know where to begin with my story. It seemed easier to say "no" and "thankbyou."

"You'll have to name 'em, you know," she said. "They can't be A and B forever."

"Yeah, I just named them."

"Ahhhhh, you being a new mama to two, it's a lot of work. Take your time."

Take my time? I didn't have time. I would be leaving tomorrow morning and had no idea what would happen.

My attorney, Richard Walton, called early in the morning and the first thing he said was, "They still didn't show up or call?"

"No." I shook my head. A hello would have been nice, I thought.

"Okay, you have the three choices," he said.

I had memorized them by now, but I let him repeat them anyway.

"Susan, this is *if* they don't show up by the time you leave."

"I know, thank you."

He warned me that one of the choices, the one I chose in going for full parentage myself, would be extremely difficult and might be a long road. The "difficult" part didn't worry me, the "long road" did. It wasn't fair to the babies they needed parents now, not four years from now. I wanted to go for full parentage so I could find them a good home right now, or relatively soon. Without that, it seemed like they had nothing and I knew I would bond with them if it was for too long. I didn't know what 'too long' was.

"What about being able to charge the parents with abandonment?" I asked, thinking I might have something because they did abandon their twins. "I'd bring charges against them in a minute."

"You can't do that."

"Why?"

"Any parent can leave or abandon their child at the hospital or any 'safe shelter,' which means they go to social services for care. The babies can grow up in the system if the parents want them to. Both biological parents have to legally agree to let their parental rights go before anyone else could become the parent. Some parents never sign off their parental rights, and the kids stay in the system until they are eighteen."

I was so angry after he told me that. How could it be legal? There was no way I was going to let that happen. My anger stirred a fierce part of me that made me intense and stubborn.

"Well, number one and two are out of the question," I said.

"I will not put them into social services and I already co-parent with my ex and joint custody is a nightmare. I can't imagine co-parenting with the intended father, who has other issues, especially after Michael wanted me to run away with him. It's going to have to be fight for parentage, if they even put up a fight." The twins stirred when I raised my voice.

"Okay, but I'm warning you, there is a very good chance you will not win."

I was flustered. His voice sounded fierce like he was not invested in helping me, but I would do what I thought was right, regardless of whether he was there or not. I figured I might be going to bat alone and had to prepare myself. "But I might win, and if I don't at the very least I know I tried." My biggest worry was bonding with the babies. How long would it be before that happened? How long would they stay with me? What would I do if it happened? These questions continued to swim through my mind.

22

Going Home

It was a bright fall day when we left the hospital. The nurses helped me pack up baby supplies and Tracey and Lauren were on their way to pick us up. I was starving and told them I'd need to eat very soon.

Michael and Jackie never called to ask or see how the twins were doing.

I couldn't wait to hug Brian and Steven. I missed them so much. When we reached my home, Lauren pulled into our driveway. I started to get out of the car and grab the car seats. "I'm heading over to Target to get some things for the twins before the boys get home," I said.

"We've been meaning to talk to you about something," Lauren said, looking down just outside her car door as she shut it. "Let's get the babies and go inside." She said.

I thought of the last time they wanted to "talk to me about something," so I hesitated, summoning my courage. Not much could surprise me now, I thought.

"We think, well, our attorney, Tracey, and I think it would be best if we took care of the twins. I'll take Megan and Tracey will take Matthew. We have a paper we need for you to sign so we can take care of them," Lauren said.

I was stunned at the thought of them taking over, and even more shocked that they had so little confidence that I could do the job. My body got hot and I felt drained. I could feel my pad get soaked with blood. I knew they had resources that I did not—like a twenty-four hour nanny, housekeeper, and all the money in the world—but that didn't matter to me. I wondered what I could possibly say to them and struggled for a response. I heard this come out of my mouth: "Yeah, um, no. That won't work for me. They're staying here with us. I will not sign anything for you take them away from me."

"We don't want you to get too attached, Susan," Tracey said. "You have a lot of hormones going on right now and we want things to be done right," Lauren said.

"No," I said loudly. It felt like they were ganging up on me and my feelings were really hurt. "*Things to be done right*" was all I heard. So that was it. They were worried that I would get too attached. The truth was, I didn't know if I would get attached or not, but I wasn't letting them go, I was a big part of the twins being here.

"Susan, come on," Lauren said.

"No, this has gotten out of hand. It's ridiculous. Like I said, I can use your help, but you are not taking them from my house." I felt huge, hurtful tears coming.

There was a shift in their mood at what I said, and it seemed their desire to help was gone. They left quickly, leaving me, and the car seats at the front door. It hit me hard. I wasn't ready for them to throw this one at me, and they surprised me. Again! I hadn't heard everything and it shocked me and made me feel like I couldn't trust them again. My confidence was at an all-time low. I was alone with the twins, my two boys, and my daycare kids.

I started a list of things I needed at Target. It was cold outside and I would have to bundle up the twins before I left. I made a mental list of the things I would need to buy.

Bassinets: 2

Sleepers: 6—no, say 12 (6 each)
Diaper cloths: a lot
Clothes: I have no idea
Sheets for the bassinets: 2 each
Miscellaneous: diapers, powder, diaper cream…

I felt overwhelmed again, and had no idea what I was getting into. *Fuck them,* I thought. I can do this myself. They bailed. I knew they would. Fuck, Fuck! You'd think they would have thought about this, but no, they decided to take the twins without ever asking me.

What was I going to do? The boys would be home from school soon, so I barely had enough time to go shopping. I put the car seats into my car and headed to Target with the twins. Before we left the driveway, Megan was crying for a bottle and Matthew had spit-up all over his mouth and chin. I wiped his mouth with a tissue. Megan screamed all the way on the short drive to Target, and Matthew joined her when we made it to the parking lot. With one hand, I held her bottle and put Matthew into the middle of the cart, the only place I could put them in with the car seat carriers. Then I put Megan in the cart but it wouldn't fit into the middle of the cart so I secured it into the top of the child's seat of the cart but I'd have to hold it so it'd stay secure. Now there was no room for stuff and I was one less hand holding Megan's carseat. "Fuck!" I threw the diaper bag and my purse over each shoulder and started walking, but I couldn't remember if I locked the car.

An older lady, who was probably seventy or so and wearing thin-rimmed glasses, stared at me as I passed her. I shot her an angry glance back. It must have been because I said the F-word out loud! I felt hot, like I was going to pass out. She looked like she was going to say something to me. *Please don't talk to me, please, please don't,* I thought, still fumbling with Megan's bottle.

"Do you need some help?" another older lady with beautiful gray hair asked as I tried to maneuver the cart. She didn't look as mean as the other one, but she seemed the type that wanted to help.

I smiled faintly with a meaning of please leave me alone.

"Um, I think I have it now. Thanks." I moved the cart into place so I could move forward.

"Awww, they look brand-new," she said, peering over at the twins for a good, long look. She followed me with her cart and said, "They probably shouldn't be out in this cold." It was definitely something my mother would have said.

I felt my blood pressure rise thinking I was damned if I did, and damned if I didn't.

I said nothing and smiled faintly again.

"Wow, they look nothing like you! Are you sure they are yours? Maybe they look like your husband?"

Oh. My. Fucking. God. She really wanted to know. The expectant look on her lined face waited for my answer.

I thought of all the things I could say, but said what was on my mind. "No, I don't have a husband," I said a little too loudly. I held my left hand up and said, "See, no ring." I wiggled my fingers. I managed to take a deep breath and added my most meaningful response. "I gave birth two days ago as a surrogate mother, and the parents changed their minds and walked out on us. They don't want their healthy twins."

Her eyes widened, and she gave me a quick once-over like I was crazy.

She was probably right. I felt a little crazy and I had zero fucks left to give.

She eased her cart away from mine and glared at me. I was sure she might call security thinking maybe I stole the twins. I got those looks a lot lately, and that face full of uncertain emotion I knew well. I hoped no one else would ask me questions, because I was afraid I might start screaming, crying, or both.

I moved through Target as fast as I could, grabbing a bunch of stuff that fit into the cart while turning my mental list around in my mind. I had forgotten my list at home. I heard a baby cry a few aisles over and my breasts tingled. My anxiety felt overwhelming, and I thought about my milk coming in. My body wanted to nurse, but my mind fought it, and then the tingling turned into pain and my breasts throbbed along with my legs. Dr. Kazman had given me a pill to dry up my milk, but I didn't remember where it was. I felt wet on my chest and looked down into my jacket at my shirt and saw two little wet spots over my hard nipples that were quickly growing bigger.

I'd have to come back for the bassinets because I had no room and no more money for all the extra things, including the fluffy pillows I wanted for feeding the babies. I could use my own pillows, I decided.

As I was getting ready to check out, I realized I forgot the diapers, the most important thing, but I knew I had enough from the hospital to last me until I headed back for the bassinets, so I stayed in line.

The lady at the cash register was wonderful, ushering us through quickly. "Boy, you have your hands full," she said. I somberly laughed inside.

She spared me any personal questions I wasn't able to handle. At that point I had just enough time to get back to the house, pick up the boys and the daycare kids, change my shirt, and stuff toilet paper in my bra. I was so grateful the school was across the street from the house. I grabbed the car seats in each arm and headed across the street.

The boys were excited to see the twins but they looked hesitant because of what I said to them about getting too close to the twins. I could tell they wanted to love them up. My heart broke in a million pieces when the boys cooed the twins and put their little cheeks up to their tiny faces. The daycare kids did the same, and then we went about our afternoon doing homework, having snacks, and talking. The kids teased the dogs and they barked, which woke the twins.

Terrie came home as the daycare kids were starting to leave with their moms, who all came at different times and stayed to hear about my journey with the twins from the beginning. They all knew I was a surrogate mother, but still couldn't believe what happened. Seeing the twins took on a whole new meaning. Terrie looked at me knowing exactly where I was in way of handling things and went over to see the twins. "Welcome to our family, Megan and Matthew," she said.

Once the boys were fed and in bed, I managed to get the twins to sleep at the same time.

"Ter, I have to go back to Target and get two bassinets for beds. Would you mind keeping an eye on the kids for me? I don't want them sleeping in my bed tonight and I shouldn't be more than an hour."

"Sure, no problem," she said.

Four hundred dollars later I made it home with the heavy baby goods.

Lauren called the next day, saying she and Tracey had second thoughts and now were willing to help without taking possession of the babies. No doubt she had talked to her lawyer. After my first full twenty-four hours of taking care of the twins alone, I was open to any help I could get. I was still mad, so I was on guard with both of them.

"When will the court dates start?" I asked.

"Richard filed the case, and we paid the court fees, but we haven't heard back yet. Probably not until after the new year."

I prepared myself for the worst, thinking we wouldn't hear anything until January.

All we could do was wait.

23

Under The Pepper Tree

The twins were nine days old and their parents still hadn't called or showed up. It happened to be two days after my fortieth birthday, but it felt like it should have been my seventieth. Sleep had become a thing of the past, and my post labor bleeding had gotten heavier. I was soaking extra-large pads every fifteen to twenty minutes and I didn't feel like I was recovering from my labor. I wondered if it was normal for a twin delivery.

I knew it wasn't normal.

That day the clouds folded over in an overcast sky. The cool air was wet with dew dripping from the trees as I dropped Brian and Steven off at school. I must have looked as white as a ghost, walking blindly across the street back toward the house, not aware of my surroundings or any cars going by. I needed to call Dr. Kazman to see what to do about my bleeding, but that would require an office visit that I didn't have time for. Overnight I'd saturated a few of the big disposable pads the hospital had given me and had none left. I needed more, but getting any required a trip to the store. I wondered how much money I had left in my checking account.

Once home, I sat down on the couch and opened the drapes to watch the murky fog drift by in the window of our living room. I concentrated on my breath when I realized I couldn't feel or see my chest going in or out. My breathing was coming in short, rapid, shallow panicked breaths.

I put my head back on the couch and tried to imagine drifting in space to calm myself and thought about how stars burn out once their core turns into iron. I, too, was burning out. What would I become?

Lauren and Tracey were coming over soon with the twins. They'd taken the twins for the night so I could rest. I was having trouble getting them on a synced schedule. One twin would sleep, the other would cry. One would feed and the other cried or the two cried together. Once in a while I got them to sleep at the same time, but it never lasted more than twenty minutes. I couldn't get them on a schedule for the life of me and couldn't get myself on one either. I felt like a failure and still had to take care of my boys and the after school daycare kids.

Even though I didn't have them last night, I couldn't sleep. I missed them like a mother would. I wanted to love the twins like my own, but my heart fought the reasoning of my mind. It was the only thing I knew how to do naturally, be a mother.

I heard a soft knock at the front screen door and saw Adam through the half-closed front door. He knew there was a chance I'd be alone because we talked the night of my birthday over the phone. I pulled myself up and went to the door.

"Is this a good time or…"

"No, it's fine," I said and opened the screen. "I have a little bit of time before Lauren and Tracey come over with the twins." I hadn't seen him for a few months, so when I let him in, he put his arms out and held me close. Finally, he was here when I needed him most. It felt so good to be in his arms.

Instead of telling me everything was going to be okay, he started to rub himself up against me. He moaned and moved his body up and down mine, hard up against me. I cringed in my mind, but my stomach responded with the flutter of wounded butterfly wings.

"I'm bleeding really heavy, like heavier than any other time."

"I don't care. I'm okay with that. I know it's probably too soon after the birth, but you look great." He had a hungry look and pulled me to him while he kissed my neck.

I thought that maybe if we were together, I might feel better. Before I could figure it out, we were already in my bedroom. I felt like shit and knew I looked like it too. We fumbled around and his clothes were quickly off. He lightly tugged at my shirt and pulled my pants down. I grabbed my white old lady granny panties, embarrassed mid-way, and turned away from him to pull off my large pad full of blood. I folded it, put it on my dresser, and then turned back to him. I turned around as he spread an old blanket over my bed and I lay down on my back. He laid down alongside me and balanced his weight on one elbow, and with the other hand gently pulled my white maternity bra (the only bra that would fit) straps down one at a time, my weighty breasts freed from their cups. His face was serious and his blue-green eyes full of wonder as if he were admiring beautiful art.

His mouth covered the breast closest to him and he suckled it, unexpectedly tasting my milk. Hungrily, he sucked one and then the other as milk spilled out from the sides.

He climbed on top of me and we had sweaty, bloody, messy sex. I looked at him searching to find words to say something, but nothing came out, so I put my head back waiting for it to be over.

I felt nothing.

It was over so fast I couldn't remember when we started. He slipped and slid through me so fast I wasn't even sure my body was there. My life was completely fucked up, and I could hear the twins crying in my head. He talked but I don't remember one word he said. Not one.

He left after a short visit to the bathroom.

I was on my way to being lost—falling away from reality, and for some reason, I couldn't ask for help. I changed my pad and sat on my bed wondering what just happened and felt the blood coming out of me faster. My mind was fuzzy and my body felt heavy as if holding something deep inside, then I felt a slight wriggle between my legs.

I ran into the bathroom and sat down on the toilet where blood dripped into it like an irritating faucet drip that wouldn't stop. Instinctively, I opened my legs and felt something pushing its way out of my body without any help. I reached down and pulled up what looked like a blood clot, dirty red in color, the size of a small dirt clod in my hands.

Bewildered and shocked, I sat holding it and examining it from all sides and then I felt a stronger wriggle, like something larger burrowing its way out of my body as if all my insides were pouring out. I reached my other hand down, feeling the intensity of its coming. It entered into the world as a fist-sized blood clot that looked different than the first one. It had a whitish color throughout it. I plopped the smaller one into the toilet.

My body wept a bright blood red.

Why was this happening? What was it? Maybe I was bleeding to death. I felt dizzy at the thought and the fuzzy white feeling in my head made it feel heavy in the same way I had felt after the reduction of the triplet. The same buzzing in my ears came back hard and took over my body until I went numb.

I feebly stood holding the clot in one hand, pulling my pants up with the other.

Was it?

No, it couldn't be. Dr. Kazman said he probably got it all.

It was off-red, not a blood red, but dark carmine red.

Was I was holding the dead fetus that I pretended not to see floating around in the ultrasounds throughout my pregnancy?

Guilt and remorse saturated my numb feeling. I didn't believe what I was seeing and holding with my own hands. I felt frozen with grief.

I looked closer at the clot. It was war, and had diffuse, white color braided throughout and artfully intertwined, and could only be what I recognized as the outline of a skeleton, a backbone partially fused and disintegrated into the form of a circled clot. The doctor said it would be reabsorbed back into my body. He never said I might find it later in my own hands. I couldn't see the actual body, but I looked closer and pulled it apart to see.

I knew it was the twins' brother or sister that had been terminated at thirteen weeks, six days.

I howled like an injured animal, giving voice to, what my body felt aching inside. My breasts round and hard, waiting to nourish a child. My muscles still throbbed between my legs from giving birth, my female anatomy trying to recover, and now naturally shedding what was left of the man-made transfer of human embryos.

Deep, dark guttural cries came and tears drenched my cheeks. I felt like I had oceans worth to cry and all I knew was he or she was real, right here in my bloodied hands, and I was calling it an "it."

I fell to my knees weeping, as if praying and cradling it in my arms.

I didn't want to pray because who the hell would I be praying to? As far as I knew, the God I believed in just put a dead fetus into my hands trying to tell me what I did was wrong. Well, he was wrong, that imaginary old man in the sky. He was wrong.

The God I thought I knew wouldn't make me feel shameful, wouldn't make me beg for forgiveness. The God I wanted to know would only hold me in love and let me learn from my mistake.

Unconditional love, Goddammit. "Do you know what that is?" I screamed with my face up to the sky. A flash of my affair with Adam swept through my mind. I felt like God was reprimanding me for my affair with a pastor. Who was my God anyway? I cried harder, falling to the cold linoleum bathroom floor from my calloused knees onto my butt.

What I did was right for me, and I didn't want to apologize for it again. I faltered in my own human weakness and found myself apologizing. "I'm sorry!" I said. "So sorry, oh so sorry."

I wasn't dying, but then again I was.

Shame grabbed me and shook me hard. The life-blaming shame I knew so well.

"It" would no longer be an "it." It would now be a he. I couldn't bear to use the word "it" any longer. I pulled toilet paper from the roll, folded it neatly with one hand and put him on top of it, and then grabbed more to wipe off my bloodied hands. The aroma of blood permeated the room and seeped into my memory.

He waited to have his own birth/death/burial day.

Still crying, I made my way out into the front yard to the large pepper tree near the corner by the sidewalk. The fog crowded in as I hit my knees to make a hole in the dirt. Hundreds of school children were across the street at the elementary school. I was used to hearing them on the playground and loved the way they laughed, cried, screamed, and played. But right now it was starkly quiet. I heard myself gulp, and knew I had to be quiet or I would be discovered. I wondered if it was okay to bury something not in human form but that emerged through my body, a fetus that would have been more, but now would never be acknowledged because he wasn't born alive.

No one would ever think of this little one again except me.

My knees grew cold from the wet ground and made round wet spots on my pants that saturated through to my skin. I put him down by my side. On all fours, I dug harder and faster with my bare hands like a dog burying a bone. I wanted to make the hole bigger and climb in myself. I wanted to feel what it might be like with the dirt everywhere, in my mouth, in my eyes, and on top of my naked body. To feel the roots of the gorgeous pepper tree take hold and grow through me, in my veins and around me.

To. Hold. Me.

Feeling dirt in my bare hands propelled me back to a feeling I had when I was maybe seven or eight, when I would escape to the elementary school two blocks away from where I lived. I found a place in the tall grass, cleared out an area, and called it my thinking spot. A small stream of water flowed through it. Tall wildflowers that went up beyond my head surrounded me. So many flowers tall enough to hide in with yellow and pink petals with big black specks in the middle. There were small openings in the earthy crust filled with water making little pools of water all around me. I collected rocks and marveled at the many different kinds that I lined up around the pools of water. I'd place them on each side of the waterbed talking to myself, "black one, white one, pretty one, pebble one, crystal one, odd one," I had a name for all of them.

I ran away from home to my thinking spot many times trying to escaping my family, but mostly the stepfather, Donald. I'd sit and think in my spot for hours, reading anything I could get my hands on. I stayed there until I got so hungry I couldn't stand it. My tummy would rumble loud with hunger and I'd go home to rummage for food. No one else knew about my secret place, it was all mine. I'd lie in the earthy dirt and felt the cushioning of the sand as it formed around my little girl body. Feeling comforted, Mother Nature was all around me in my thinking spot. She was always there for me when my own mother was not.

I looked up and realized I was running out of time. I didn't want Lauren or Tracey to catch me in the yard. I didn't know if I could explain to them what happened and didn't want to. I felt fiercely protective of our time together. I thought any compassion Tracey or Lauren might feel would most likely still result in harsh judgment of me.

I took him in my hands, unwrapped the paper, and laid him into the ground. I put loose dirt on top and patted the soil with my tears sprinkling the fresh ground. "I'm so, so sorry. I'll never forget you," I whispered.

Within minutes, it felt like my grief changed me. How so I didn't know, and the realization of it seemed so simple. Life and death never felt so combined for me, coexisting so delicately. I wanted to stay in this moment, but had to get up.

Lauren pulled into the driveway. Her black suburban Lexus pulled forward then swooshed backward when she hit the brakes. It must take so much energy to always be in a hurry, and I wondered how she did that all the time. It would make me feel more frazzled.

I got up quickly, grabbed the bloodied tissue, and wiped my tears, knowing my tear-stained face was swollen. My ears buzzed and I felt like I was going to pass out, so I hung my head between my legs to catch some air, and pulled myself up and back into reality. My nails were filled with dirt and mud. I shook my arms into the air to get rid of it and wiped my wet, dirty knees with my hands before I went into the house. I made my way into the kitchen before she got out of the car. I heard the twins crying from inside it and again it felt like they were calling for me, yet I didn't feel like I had anything left to give.

I leaned into the sink and brought my hands to my face to smell the fresh mud once more before I washed them off.

They smelled of new life.

24

Christmas

Lauren brought over good news a week and a half before Christmas. "We finally have a hearing a few days after Christmas and a court date set for the second week in January, 2002." She said. "Can you believe it? Oh, also Richard did file a petition for parental rights on your behalf."

I was nervous but it felt right. I didn't know what to expect.

Lauren and Tracey had taken the twins again that night, and Lauren dropped them off that morning before work. I finally got a full night sleep. It felt so good. Things seemed to be working out with all of us taking it day by day, to see how things went to determine who took the twins.

Lauren brought in a bag of baby clothes she wanted to show me.

"Look at all these darling baby clothes," she said as she pulled them all out of the large Baby Gap bag with the hangers looped together.

Outfits spilled out of the bag one by one—cute little dresses, pink, white, and multicolor. "Can you believe it? Aren't they so cute?" Lauren's huge diamond ring caught on the lacy hem of a dress. I couldn't remember how many carats her ring had but it was probably the most flawless, beautiful ring I'd ever seen.

She carefully lifted it out of the soft baby white lace. "Fuck, goddammit." She threw the other outfits to the side, picking the lace out of her ring.

I said nothing half smiling at the absurdity of the situation. I felt embarrassed and self-conscious that I was still in my old-man pajamas while she was dressed in a short black and white wool skirt with thin black stockings and beautiful black leather boots, straight out of *Vogue*. My energy was gone. My bleeding was lighter but I still felt washed up, old, and half-numb from my encounter with Adam a week before. I adjusted my blood-soaked pad while she freed her ring from the lace.

"I can't wait to pick up Megan today," she said. "I can have her, right? About four o'clock? Jennifer is going to be so excited when she gets to dress her up in these clothes!"

"Yeah, sure," I said, wondering if I should let her take Megan again even though I knew she was taking good care of her. Something just felt off. I wondered what Jennifer's life might be like as the youngest of Lauren's children and the only girl. I found out just before 9/11 that Lauren was married to the doctor who did our first embryo transfer, Dr. Cohen. Everyone knew except for me, the surrogate.

The only reason I found out was because the boys and I ran into Lauren and Dr. Cohen at Blockbuster when we went to rent movies. I looked at him in a déjà vu way. I knew him but couldn't place this man she was holding hands with her husband, Dr. Cohen. I searched his face trying to remember where I saw him last. I asked Lauren about it the next day telling her he looked oddly familiar.

"Yes, Dr. Cohen is my husband," she admitted.

It shocked me because it was after I said to her, "I heard he's married? He is so handsome," I felt like a gabby teenager, and I was gossiping about her husband! She could have told me then, well over a year ago. I wondered about it all especially after the first transfer with Evan and how Dr. Cohen had botched that because of Tracey. Now, it fit, they all knew each other, and some more than others, I'd guessed. I did know that Tracey and Lauren were best friends. There was probably way more that I didn't know.

Back in my living room, Lauren beamed with excitement at her purchases. I wondered if she and Jennifer might be getting too close to Megan, but I didn't say anything. It did seem strange to me that she was entertaining her daughter with Megan. Maybe I was jealous.

"Jennifer told me yesterday that Megan is the sister she never had."

I cringed. And then I realized she didn't buy anything for Matthew. I felt bad knowing it was difficult for me to buy extra things for the twins.

I found myself staring at the twins while Lauren looked over her receipts. How much longer would this last? Could I just go for parentage and keep them? Every time I thought about it, it was like a puzzle piece that didn't fit. I reminded myself that I was their surrogate, not their mother. They were not my babies or anyone else's yet.

Lauren picked up the pile of clothes and put them into the bag and brought them to her car. She turned halfway around to wave goodbye. Everything she bought for Megan she kept at her house. I tried to count the times she ever held Matthew or when Tracey held Megan, which was never.

This wasn't a village raising children, this was a goddamn favorites game and sometimes it felt like we were playing house like children, but I had to play along. I couldn't do this myself, especially once we went to court.

After Lauren left, I was mad at myself for not telling her why it pissed me off. Why didn't she treat them the same? But, I didn't think she or Tracey would change. Maybe it was better this way.

Then I thought about Tracey who had an older son from another marriage and a younger daughter at home with her extremely successful entrepreneur husband. They owned a

203

beautiful home in the hill section of our small beach town, and she wasn't as interested in playing house like Lauren was. She had bigger priorities like nail appointments and massages every other night. It wasn't long before I could tell she was done with the whole thing. One night a few hours after her massage, she brought Matthew back to my front door at 10 p.m. and stood there holding him out for me when I opened the door. He was crying and I could see she'd been crying too.

"I can't do this anymore, Susan, it's too stressful. Could you take him please?" I took him to my chest and calmed him by gently rocking him.

"I take Benadryl every night to sleep, and I have to pay my housekeeper extra to have her stay overnight to help. No more of this, I'm done," she said and then left as fast as she could.

I didn't feel sorry for her. I couldn't. I didn't have a housekeeper or a multi-million-dollar home on the hill. I started to feel resentful and like things were falling apart.

After I fed the twins that night, I noticed they were trying to smile. It was so cute! They had a way of making everything better. They cooed as I played with them on the floor on their baby blanket. I felt myself getting attached to them. It was a motherly connection that I couldn't deny. I had to act fast: Human bonding was happening.

All of the days and nights pushed into one another except this one. It was the twins' first Christmas. The boys and I loved Christmas. I adored watching them with the twins. I'll never forget seeing them open their presents with Terrie, and myself, looking on while taking care of the twins. Brian and Steven were so proud because they'd bought a big infant toy the twins could play with.

I'd become somewhat of an expert taking care of and feeding twins—one in my arms the other on my legs. I moved them up to my face and their newborn baby smell washed over me. I couldn't snuggle enough and so I put my nose to their little heads as much as possible.

We were are all getting dangerously close to the twins, each loving them in our own ways. I could feel it and knew my kids were feeling it, too.

My maternal instincts had always been loyal and natural, but now I felt they were lying to me. I was the mother. I wasn't the mother. It was a source of constant confusion.

I feared as a mother this whole situation with the twins was something that would hurt me all of my life. I thought about the third baby and felt guilt beyond what I thought possible. I stuffed the hurt down deeper into my body where I might not find it so easily. It had to go somewhere.

I started wondering what would happen in the courtroom in three days. Would Michael and Jackie change their minds and take the twins? Would I win parentage? There were so many unanswered questions.

I was up each night before the hearing unable to sleep. I was sweating at the thought of giving up the twins, waiting for court dates, waiting for someone to make a decision. Waiting for everything and nothing at the same time.

All I could remember was the promise I made to them. "Don't worry, I will take care of you and find you a mommy and a daddy."

Richard Walton said the first court hearing was a formality. It was a way for the judge to get familiar with the case and see who was participating and who was not. Most importantly, Richard said, "The judge needs to know all of the players."

The day of the hearing was a calm and cool winter morning. Tracey and Lauren had arranged for Lauren's housekeeper to look after the twins. I sat in the back seat as we drove to the courthouse. Richard was able to schedule morning court times so I could still watch my after-school kids. The meeting was to be informal in the judge's chambers at Edelman Children's Court in Monterey Park and part of the Los Angeles Superior Court System.

When we arrived, Richard and I headed to the judge's chambers and Lauren and Tracey waited in the lobby.

"The only reason I'm representing you is because I felt you were treated unfairly," he said. "So remember, we need to keep this as professional as possible. Just follow my lead."

I looked at him wondering what he really meant. I shrugged off the comment and kept walking with him.

We were ushered by the head bailiff to sit on the left side of the courtroom at a front table instead of going to the judge's chambers.

Michael was already there on the right side of the table, but no Jackie. I heard her voice from what sounded like a telecom. I wondered if we were late, feeling cold and empty. However, I was shocked and surprised that Michael had shown up. The judge, who had gray thinning hair on the sides and top was already seated. He seemed somewhat somber, or maybe I just felt that way.

"Why aren't you here to represent yourself in this matter, Ms. Fletcher?" the judge said to Jackie in a demanding tone.

"I don't want them, I don't want any more children. I have one that I am taking care of full-time, and I have already divorced Michael. I ask that you relieve me of this burden."

"Relieve you of the burden?" I mumbled. I let out a gasp.

"I will not relieve you of this case because you are an intricate part of the decision to bring these children into the world," the judge said. He moved paper around on his desk. "In other words, you are fifty percent responsible and will remain so throughout these hearings. You don't have to show up, but you will be present via telecom."

I hung my head, remembering when I had second thoughts about being a surrogate for them. I wished I had told Michael and Jackie absolutely not, but on the other hand I was happy the twins were here. I looked over at Michael, who looked distraught, unshaven, and unkempt. When he looked at me, I wanted to cry, unsure if it was because of what was happening or the fact that he never asked about the twins. Did he even care? He was physically present, but far, far away.

Jackie tried to say something to the judge, but her voice faded in and out.

"Yes, Ms. Fletcher, you were saying?" the judge asked.

"Well, yes, please have Susan Ring do as she is told, and send the children to social services. She's done her job and they can work out the money owed to her later. Michael will pick them up when he is financially and emotionally stable."

I hated her. Really *hatedherhatedherhatedher*. What she said wasn't even in the form of a question. It was a direct order.

The judge looked at me. "Ms. Ring?" he asked. I was motionless, frozen.

"Absolutely not, Your Honor. No!" I said feeling strong in my resolve. I was not going to let her push me around. I knew whom I was fighting for, and why.

"That's it for today," the judge said, and slammed down his gavel.

A week later the twins had a regular post-birth visit with a pediatrician, it was a friend of Lauren's. All all the twins' medical bills were still going under my medical insurance. I paid the co-pay that day and left the office thinking about the next day—our first court appearance. I would have to face Michael again and hear Jackie's voice over the phone. I didn't think I could hold it together much longer. I was so tired, and barely pulled things together for my own kids. All I wanted was to sleep, just for a little while, by myself.

While driving home from the doctor, I felt myself starting to fall asleep and not paying full attention to the road. Matthew started to cry from the back seat, and I shuddered knowing Megan would soon chime in.

I pulled into a Starbucks parking lot about a mile from

home and soothed Matthew while Megan was still fast asleep. I took their car seats out of the car and toted both of them through the parking lot but soon realized I couldn't open the door with two car seats in my hand. I put one car seat down and grabbed for the door, and then felt grateful when someone came and opened it for me.

"Thank you."

The man nodded and smiled warmly.

I couldn't remember Starbucks' fancy drink options, so I looked for the drink with the most caffeine. I put the twins down beside me and remembered I had no cash in my wallet, so I fumbled around and handed the cashier my credit card. "A coffee with the most caffeine in it but not super strong," I said. If there was such a thing, I thought.

"A tall double espresso mocha, maybe?" he asked.

"Sure, okay." He swiped my card, but it was declined. He handed it back to me with a sorry face and I fell into myself with embarrassment.

"Sorry, ma'am," the young man said.

I wanted that coffee so bad. I went for my change purse, but didn't have enough quarters, just a lot of dimes and pennies. I felt flustered and hot, like I was going to pass out again. I held onto the counter and looked down at the twins to take a moment to breathe.

"Um, okay...let me see if I have another card," I said, wondering if another one would work. I couldn't remember which one I used for the twins' doctor appointment.

A man behind me tapped my shoulder and said, "It's okay, let me buy it for you."

I looked back straight into his eyes and said, "Thank you." I noticed a long line forming behind him. I felt a flood of embarrassment and shame go through my body.

I managed to throw everything back into my purse and threw my sunglasses back on, sobbing while I made my way over to pick up my coffee. I tried hard to ignore my sadness. I felt many eyes on me, most trying to get a glimpse of the twins.

At the pick-up counter, I couldn't pick up my coffee with both hands full of car seats. I let out a muffled sob, put the twins down by a table close by, carefully grabbed my hot coffee, and walked back over. Megan stirred, but Matthew was fast asleep. I sat down and rocked her car seat. I thought about how Lauren and Tracey were only helping because they didn't want to get sued. They were covering their own asses. Though I was grateful, that they came this far to help, most of all with my boys because that's what mattered to me most. I couldn't shake the feeling that they were doing it because of what happened with Michael and Jackie. But I wished they were doing it because they wanted to, not because they felt they had to. I considered asking them for financial assistance, but I was too proud to ask. It left a bitter taste in my mouth. I never asked them for anything, and they never offered.

I had trouble asking for help with anything. I was so independent and it never helped me. My biggest question was how much longer was it all going to take?

I looked at the twins. Both of them were wide-eyed, curiously watching me quietly, smiling.

I melted.

25

First Court Date

On our first official court date, Michael was surrounded by a handful of attorneys, which made me feel like I lost before we started. They all stood in nice suits around him, listening to his story in the lobby of the courtroom, which was huge and had about twenty round islands with fixed seats in a circle that fit about ten to fifteen people at a time in each one. There was a lot of room and families watched as their kids ran back and forth from pod to pod. Windows surrounded the room with panoramic views of the mountains. I could hear Michael talking from where I sat and leaned over to hear what he was saying. When I peered over, he lifted his arm showing the attorneys how one of the planes went into the twin towers on 9/11.

"It just exploded. I can't handle anything else right now, this is more than enough," he said.

The attorneys looked over at me and then walked him to another area of the Children's Lobby Courtroom, where the carpet was full of bright blue swirling designs and the walls were decorated with colorful children's paintings.

I recognized one of Michael's entourage as a high-profile surrogacy attorney who worked with a popular clinic in Los Angeles that celebrity clients often went to. I didn't think he worked outside the surrogacy clinic. I felt alone sitting by myself. Richard was talking to another attorney in the hallway, and Tracey and Lauren sat at another island close to the front door.

One of the attorneys pulled away from the group Michael was in and started to walk toward me. Thirty-something, she had long, semi-curly brunette hair and was dressed in a high-quality navy suit with a red silk shirt and gorgeous matching high heels. She approached me smiling, fixed herself right in front of my knees, and put one hand on her hip. "What makes you think you have any parental right to the twins you gave birth to?" she said.

I immediately wondered where in the world she got the audacity to talk to me like that. Like a fierce mother tiger protecting her cubs I said, "I suggest you talk to your client and find out why. If anyone thinks that I am going to stand by and watch the twins be taken to social services, they are dead wrong." I stared back at her.

I felt my blood pressure rise. I squirmed in my seat feeling awkward dressed in my fat pants because nothing else fit yet. She glared at me and went back to her circle without another word. I felt profoundly comfortable with my motherly instinct protecting the twins. I watched her go back and whisper into another attorney's ear. He looked back at me and whispered back to her. I'm sure they were trying to assess what kind of a person I was and what my motive might be.

Richard came back to sit by me and asked what the woman said to me. I told him.

"This isn't looking good, Susan," he said with a deep sigh. "They are all talking about how Michael deserves his fatherhood regardless of the contract. They are his children." He sat down next to me.

"I know that, but you know the circumstances."

"The contract is a civil matter and doesn't weigh in with family law. I can tell they want to represent Michael, but he isn't making it easy. He's proving to be unstable," Richard said. I looked over again and saw that he was looking rattled. There wasn't anything I could do about his problems. I needed to protect the twins.

The first court date yielded nothing. No decisions were made and the next court date was set for the second week of January.

Within the next three or four court dates, Lauren or Tracey drove to the courthouse each time and waited in the lobby for me. I would be in the courtroom sometimes for four to five hours. I was told later that the court was trying very hard to give Michael the benefit of the doubt, to reach out for his children and take responsibility, but he didn't.

The only change in those few weeks was the court-appointed an attorney to represent the twins. The new attorney's name was Jim Denson.

I continued to wonder how long this could go on. My bonding was intensifying and I didn't know what to do about it. I often waited alone as everyone talked and walked around me. I tried to keep it together, but I felt like things were slipping away little by little.

Things were changing, but not in my favor. The court had called in social services to assess the situation. During one court appearance, Richard pointed to an older woman with gray hair in a bun. "That's the woman from social services," he said. I pictured a group of social services people coming to the house to take the twins away. I couldn't let that happen. I asked Richard if it was possible.

"Anything is possible at this point, Susan," he said and then cleared his throat.

Pictures filled my mind of the twins going from guardian to guardian, foster parent to foster parent, house to house until Michael was ready for them. I doubted they'd even stay together. The thought of it happening broke my heart.

I became upset and wondered what I could do next. My

first thought was to take off to Mexico with the twins, but I would need to take my kids with me too, and that would put them in harm's way. I wasn't willing to do that. I thought about the boys' dad standing at my screen door wondering where his sons were while I fled to Mexico. I didn't even speak Spanish.

The courts were unprepared because there was no precedent. Not only that, but it couldn't keep up with science. Nothing like this had ever happened. There were no laws governing surrogacy. The twins had me as their surrogate mother fighting for them and a father who couldn't care for them, and never made any attempt to see how they were doing. But he still showed up for court. As far as I knew Jackie was still participating in the court appearances via telecom. It made me feel better to know she couldn't get out of the situation that easily, even though I knew she still didn't want the twins.

A scowling older woman with gray thinning hair sat by Michael in the lobby at one of our court appearances. She was petite with a round, full face. She wore glasses and looked mad at the world, and she made every effort to stare me down every time I looked at her. I had no idea who she was.

"Michael's mother is here," Richard told me as he covered his mouth.

I felt shocked, mortified, and happy at the same time. She finally showed up. Maybe Michael's brother and his wife might step in as well, which wouldn't be too bad. If his family became involved, maybe that would be a good thing. Michael's family certainly had the financial resources to care for the twins. His brother was an executive for a Fortune 500 company, and I knew his mother had a large home in Beverly Hills, so this could work out for the twins. But they would have to show that they wanted the twins, and the biggest problem was that Michael never made a strong claim for his own children.

We left the courtroom again with nothing resolved. I felt sad and would only rest when I knew the twins were safe and loved. The only safe place right now was with me.

The boys were still at school when I got home from court. I kept trying to think of someone who could help me sort this legal mess out, someone I could call, but no one had an answer for me. I cuddled Matthew close and kissed his sweet little face, and then he smiled his first real smile. I reached down to coo and kiss Megan and I got a half smile from her. They were reaching milestones without their Mommy and Daddy. Tears fell down my cheeks and my breasts ached. My body was still shedding blood but it was lighter. I was losing weight fast.

The twins were two months old and smiling. I felt myself getting closer to them, so I knew I had to do something very soon. It was getting too late for me, and I worried I might not be able to let go.

The phone rang.

"Hello?"

"Hello, is this Susan Ring?" a woman said.

"Yes, it is."

"My name is Yvette Sloan from Channel 7 news. I've heard from a reliable source that you are a surrogate mother and the intended parents you had backed out on you and twins you gave birth to. Are they there at home now with you?"

I froze, unable to breathe. My first instinct was to deny it all, so I did.

"No, I have no idea what you are talking about. You must have the wrong Susan Ring," I said.

I slammed down the phone and my heart raced, wondering if they knew where I lived and if news trucks would show up at the door. Who called the media? I doubted it was Lauren or Tracey because they were more afraid of the media than I was. The only ones who could have leaked the story were people at the boys' school. I had told a few of the teachers what happened because I'd taken the twins across the street many times when I picked up the kids at school, and there were many media connections in this small town. Having the media involved was the last thing I wanted, because if I told my story, the twins would become everyone's twins, which would delay things even more.

Who was I kidding? I had no idea who called them. A lot of people knew about my situation.

New fears about the media clouded my mind at the next court date. Michael's attorneys were gone. He was representing himself, which I felt was a horrible idea because he never assumed his parentage. His mother, a blood relative to her infant grandchildren, wasn't there. He sat alone, and I almost felt sorry for him. I gulped hard.

"Michael's family does not want to take on the responsibility for the twins," Richard announced. His sky blue eyes looked tender and dumbfounded. He pushed back his sandy blonde hair, unbuttoned his suit jacket, and sat down looking defeated.

I was sorrowful that Michael's family did not back him and would not take responsibility for the twins.

Another social services woman entered the courtroom and joined the first one.

Things were moving fast, but I wasn't sure which way the courts would go. On one hand, I was worried that social services would come to the house and take the twins. On the other, I feared I would be inundated with news media outside my home. I was panicked and had to come up with something or feared things could only get worse.

I walked out of the courtroom and into the lobby to let Lauren and Tracey know about the family.

"The family won't assume any responsibility for the twins."

"Fuckers!" Lauren said. She pushed back her perfect hair on both sides.

"What are we going to do?" Tracey asked. "Fuck!"

"I don't know, but I know I am not going to let them go to social services, you guys, no matter what happens," I said, certain that I would do anything for them.

Jim Denson, the attorney for the twins, walked over to me. "Susan, can I have a word for a minute?"

"Sure."

We walked away together toward the courtroom lobby and stood by the window. He looked at me very intently.

"This is off the record. If I give my recommendation that you take the twins, will you adopt them out to a hopeful family?" he asked. His looked serious. I knew the court was more in favor of adopting the twins out over letting me keep them. But if they made me the legal mother, I could legitimately keep them, something that had never been done in surrogacy with no biological ties.

"Well, yeah, that is my intention, Jim," I said, my voice quivering. "I feel myself bonding with them now more than ever. I need help here, but yes, that is my intention."

"Okay, I'm going back before the judge to give my recommendation to the court that you become their natural and legal mother in the state of California and against their biological father. All I have is your word, Susan."

"Okay..." I was excited but didn't know what Jim's recommendation might resolve.

"Come into the courtroom with me so we can get things moving."

I followed him gladly. Jim was the first one who trusted me and felt like I did about resolving the matter.

The judge took Jim's recommendation into consideration but did not make a judgment that day, which meant the court would only consider it.

Jim, Richard, and I met outside the courtroom in the lobby to talk further.

"The court is having a difficult time making a decision in this case because the father has every right to his children," Jim said. "The twins may end up in social services until he gets better."

"No they won't," I said, my eyes welling with tears. "Richard you asked me earlier if Michael signed over his parental rights to me, would I give up what is owed to me on my surrogacy contract? Remember? I said yes without hesitation. Why exactly were you asking me that question? What did you hope to accomplish?" I asked.

"I thought maybe Michael would let go of his parental rights if he didn't have to pay you the balance of your contract and everything else. He still hasn't made any statement that says he wants his children. I'm not sure he is all there, but at the very least, he has to say he wants them." He shifted his weight onto his other leg and sat down at a pod.

"I think the 9/11 tragedy has hit us all in an emotional way," Jim said, letting out a big sigh as he sat down by Richard. I joined them.

"So what do you think would persuade him to sign over his rights? Does he care at all or is he just not able to take care of himself, let alone the twins with no help?" I said.

"What are you getting at, Susan?" Jim asked.

"Maybe it's all about the money right now," I said softly. They both looked at me. "Well, Richard's question got me thinking." I tapped the pen on my journal. "Michael and Jackie breached our contract, right?"

"Right. We already know that, Susan," Richard said sounding exhausted and then added, "And Michael never gave me an answer when I asked him that question, so maybe it's not off the table yet."

"Maybe I need to bring a lawsuit against Michael and Jackie for breach of contract? Maybe then they will change their minds," I said boldly, knowing I had to do what I had been thinking about for some time now.

Jim raised his eyebrows and looked over at Richard.

"Do you think the twins will go to DCFS, Jim?" I asked, getting up to stand in front of him.

"It's possible, I couldn't say for sure," he said.

I kept pushing. "Do you think it's highly possible?"

"Yes, I do." He looked at me and said, "But, Susan, that might not be a good idea right now. Maybe you and Richard need to discuss it further."

Richard looked away from us and said, "No way, it's not a good idea." I couldn't tell if it really wasn't a good idea or he didn't like that it came from me.

"I can't wait any more," I said. "Neither of you go home to the twins every day and look at their sweet little faces and cuddle them like a parent would. It's not fair to keep going like this, and not fair for them to be placed with DCFS as infants."

"If we get a private party to assess his mental health, everything will get held up in the court system. Maybe we can get medical records from his present doctors?" Jim offered, leaning into our conversation.

We nodded at each other. I got up and then sat back down thinking I didn't have anything else to lose.

"Richard, let me ask you this…" I said.

"What?" He wouldn't look at me.

"I've decided to sue Michael and Jackie for breach of contract in civil court. I can do that, right?"

He looked at me like I had lost my mind. "Yes, but I do not advise it," he said sternly.

"Why?" I put my journal down on the cushion.

"It won't make you look very good in the eyes of the court. It will make you appear money hungry." He said the last three words slowly.

"I don't care, we have to do something. I can't keep going this way, day and night. I get some help from Lauren and Tracey, but I can't keep doing this. It's breaking me."

"I do not advise it," Richard said and looked away.

He wasn't going to budge, and I wasn't going to wait. This whole time in court I'd been listening to my gut, aware of my instincts and trying to know what was best for the twins. Even through fear of the unknown I waited, listened, and watched. It was time to make a move.

"Okay, thank you for your advice." I looked at my watch. "I've got to go get the twins and my daycare kids. Talk to you guys later." I moved away from the pod and went over to Tracey and Lauren near the front door.

"Let's go," I said heading for the door.

"What's up?" Tracey asked.

"What's going on, Susan?" Lauren asked, grabbing her keys and purse.

"I'll tell you on the way home. I have something to talk to you two about."

26

Taking Over

The sky hung gray and dark, and it was raining hard on the way home from court. I looked out the window and watched the rainfall dance down the window as the drops hit and separated into patterns, disappearing into the black folds outside the door. I thought about all the possible rain traffic delays, which meant dead stop traffic in L.A. I filled Lauren and Tracey in with what happened in court and they agreed, it was the best idea we'd come up with to force a response. When I mentioned that Richard advised against it, they both looked worried. I was worried too, but we had to do something.

"I'll call Desmond Browne, our family attorney, when I get home," Tracey said. "I'm sure he will take the civil case to sue their asses." All of a sudden she hit the brakes of her car hard to avoid hitting the car in front of us. We slid a few feet on the wet pavement and barely missed the car in front of us.

"Jesus, Tracey!" Lauren yelled.

"I'll get all the paperwork ready of all things he will probably need," Lauren said with a heavy sigh. She turned around to me in the backseat. "Are you sure you should be doing this if Richard said not to?"

"I don't have a choice, Lauren. Michael and Jackie have pushed this, not me. We'll soon see if it's all about money."

It fell quiet for the rest of our ride home. Usually one of us had something to say, but the quiet was nice for a change.

"What if we go to your house and the media is waiting?" Tracey said as we turned the corner to my house. "I'll keep driving if I see one media van. I swear I will."

I pictured it and cringed. "That would screw up everything, plus I told them they had the wrong number and I didn't know what they were talking about."

"They have ways of knowing, Susan, trust me," Tracey said.

There was no media in front of the house, thank God, so they dropped me off. I barely made it home to get the kids from school.

Lauren called me later that day to let me know that Desmond Browne was on board to file a civil lawsuit against Michael and Jackie. He would file for an undisclosed amount for punitive damages, so I forwarded my surrogacy contract with the names and addresses of Michael and Jackie. Desmond told us they would be served the next day.

Good, I thought. The twins were two and a half months old and getting big so fast. I remembered when my boys were that little. The time goes so fast, yet so slow. I didn't know if I would hear back from Michael and Jackie, but regardless, this was what I had to do. Knowing Jackie and the fact that the lawsuit revolved around money, my bet was that we'd hear back from them.

The next day was Friday. After a hard rain, it was a crisp, clean new day with white puffy clouds drifting over and spreading throughout the sky. I spent the day taking care of the twins, who were getting too big for all their clothes. The boys came home and the daycare kids followed into the house to get a snack and do homework. I didn't have any extra time like I did before the twins.

I was sure Michael and Jackie had been served by now.

When my phone rang, I hesitated wondering if they were calling. It was Lauren, telling me they'd been served with the lawsuit. A peace fell over me that it would soon all be resolved. Not easy, but at the very least, resolved to move on.

I turned the lights on in the house under a dark evening sky and started preparing dinner after the daycare kids left. And then the phone rang.

"Hello?"

"Susan, it's Jackie." Her voice was bothered and angry. "Why in the hell did you pull this on us?"

"You can stop right there, Jackie. I'm not going to argue with you or Michael." I wanted so badly to say a few other choice words, but I knew I'd get nowhere telling her what I really thought.

"Michael is on the other line, so he knows what is going on," Jackie said. I turned off the stove and went into my bedroom for privacy. The boys were watching cartoons and the twins were sleeping soundly in my room. Terrie would be home soon.

"Hello," Michael said, sounding calm and relaxed.

"What do you want?" I asked as I moved to the bed to get comfortable and then stood up again ready for a confrontation.

"Well, you haven't done what we wanted, Jackie yelled, "and now you have brought this lawsuit against us and..." I pulled the phone away from my ear because all I could hear was her screaming.

"Calm down, Jackie," Michael said.

She signed heavily. "They are his kids, Susan. You are nothing but a kidnapper."

"I could say so many things to that comment, Jackie, but I'm not coming down to your level. Just tell me what you want. Tell me how you can make this better. Tell me how is it that I've given birth to two of your children, and they are living with me. Why?"

"We've run into some problems. I've divorced Michael and I've moved to Boston with Evan. Michael needs to get his life together, but he can't take the twins because he can't even take care of himself."

"How is that my problem, Jackie? I've heard it all before. How is it the twins' problem? I've tried to work with you and you wouldn't even return my phone calls. How dare you? Do not try and turn this around on me."

Michael interrupted. "Jackie and I will give up our parental rights *if* you drop this lawsuit and everything else, including all we owe you and any future or pending lawsuits against us."

I started to cry. Megan began to stir and whimper with her nose scrunched up. She needed to be changed. I didn't know what to say to them and wasn't so sure I wanted to say anything. I wanted to say, *Well, let me think about it,* but decided against it. I wanted to let them know how much hurt they put into all of our lives. I wanted them to feel what I'd gone through, but I knew Jackie wouldn't understand any of it. Megan started to cry.

"Do you hear that?" I said. "Your daughter is crying and you aren't here to pick her up and hold her. The daughter you created, you wanted."

Silence.

My cry grew bigger when I started to say what I really felt. I wanted them to hurt.

"I think the biggest hurt I've had through this whole thing is that both of you have never, ever asked about the twins. You didn't ask how many fingers and toes they had when they were born. You didn't ask how much they weighed. You didn't ask anything. How can you do that? How can you not even ask?"

Megan's cry became louder than my own and then Matthew started in. Michael and Jackie said nothing.

"Yes, I'll give up the precious lawsuit and drop everything else, but I'll never forgive you for what you've done because I will never understand how you both could have done such a thing to us."

The twins' crying was too loud to hear anything else. I just let them cry because sometimes it was okay to cry. I wasn't sure Michael and Jackie heard what I said, so I screamed into the phone, "Yes," and hung up.

Terrie walked in and looked at all of us. It looked like she wasn't sure where to go first. She reached out to me and we hugged, making me feel a tremendous sense of relief. The twins were still screaming. Terrie picked up Megan and I picked up Matthew. Brian and Steven walked into the room to see what was going on.

"They are giving up their parental rights *if* I give up the lawsuit," I said through my sobs.

"That's great, Susan. Finally." She hugged me again with the kids in our arms. I called Tracey and Lauren to let them know what Michael and Jackie said. Though they weren't as overjoyed as I was, they felt the same way I did. Yet, nothing was over until it was over officially with signatures. I didn't trust Michael and Jackie to keep their word, so I knew not to get my hopes up too high.

Monday rolled around and we had one more court date to officially relieve Michael and Jackie of their parental rights. Lauren contacted Desmond Browne to let him know that I'd given up the civil lawsuit, but told him to hold on until it was all over in the courthouse. Lauren told me he was livid about it.

"Susan, these people need to pay for what they've done," he said to me on the phone. "Please rethink your decision and continue this lawsuit. At least think about it, and decide later."

"I know Desmond, they do, but I never intended to take it to the bank. I just want to give the twins a home. I started this whole thing as a surrogate mother, and didn't do it to make a family for myself. It would take too much time to punish Michael and Jackie this way." I knew he wanted to take it all the way, but I couldn't do it. We'd run out of time and we were all bonding with the twins. I didn't think anyone realized that fact more than me.

Richard Walton called after he read a copy of the civil lawsuit and I updated him.

"It's good, Susan, but it's not over yet. You didn't set a precedent, but you did what was best for the twins." He sounded happy, but I assumed he might have wanted the same thing Desmond did, to take it to a higher court and set a legal precedent. I didn't care to make a name for myself. I just wanted to get the twins a mother and father as soon as possible, and now that looked like a possibility.

Lauren called after Richard did and said it was time to look at the forty applications from couples who were interested in adopting the twins in a private adoption. Lauren and Tracey had been working behind the scenes contacting agencies and attorneys about the possibility of adoption. We couldn't do anything until the court case was over, but they had forty eager couples ready through several different private parties.

"So, Susan, you'll need to decide who will be the twins' parents," Lauren said, excited.

How in the hell was I supposed to pick parents for them? The thought was overwhelming. What if I picked wrong? I sure didn't do well with the intended parents, and my own childhood was way less than average. What if something terrible happened to them like my own childhood? What then? There was no way I could get to know a couple well enough, and there wasn't enough time before I was able to choose them.

So, how could I choose? What qualified me, and what should I look for in picking parents? There was no way of knowing who would serve best as parents. Everything I thought of made me wonder if I was the right one to choose, and I was tired.

"What do you think, Susan?" Lauren asked.

"I don't know. I just want to sleep through a whole night and not wake up once."

"Well, we have to get going with this."

"Okay, well go ahead and pick the top five couples, and we can go from there. The twins need to be changed, so I'll talk to

27

Giving Up Gray

Behind the longing to sleep through the whole night was the urge to be held again in Adam's arms. I'd talked to him on the phone over the past few weeks while I was taking care of the twins, but I only had time to see him once. I thought about my physical desire to get lost in his touch again, but I knew the only real "love" he was ever able to give me was human touch, and that was sporadic at best.

For a person who knew me better than most, he was never there when I really needed him. For a secret friend, that sucked, and I started to wonder why I was seeing him at all. The emotional connection I felt with him ebbed and flowed. Sometimes his touch was enough, but this time it wasn't.

I know we made love in the past by how it felt to me. They way we moved together, how we looked at each other. He said the L word maybe twice in all those years together. When he said, "I love you Susan" the first time, I could tell by the look on his face afterwards that he felt he probably shouldn't have said it. It was in the moment, but I held onto it like they were the last words I'd ever hear him say to me. Whenever he gave me a card for my birthday, or Valentines Day or some other holiday, it always said, "Love, Me" sometimes "Love, Adam." But never,

"I love you." I loved him but didn't push for more because it always took us out of where we were in our relationship. When I couldn't stand it anymore, and wanted more in a relationship, I'd break up with him. Sometimes it'd be for a few days, weeks, for months, and sometimes a year or two at a time.

This time I needed more for myself. I deserved more. The last time we saw each other wasn't good for either of us. I still held onto anything and everything about our affair, but most of the time it was with a nearly invisible string.

Why did I keep trying to make it something? Love maybe? I fell in love with my lover early on, but he didn't add to my life or return my love. Love was a bitch and blind, as far as I was concerned, because you can't see a thing when you give your heart away.

The hard truth was he was convenient and sometimes fit my needs.

Once in a great while when we felt bold, we'd talk of him leaving his wife. He was sure the only job he'd ever get after the board of directors at the church threw him out as pastor would be flipping hamburgers at McDonald's. I pictured him in that role and it made me laugh out loud.

Would I even want him *if* he left his wife? This was a break-through moment for me. My answer was *no*.

It occurred to me that now I might have the chance to have a real relationship. The one I'd always wanted and dreamed of. I decided to give myself time to be by myself and get stronger. I didn't need Adam to make my life better. In fact, our secret relationship made me feel worthless because I knew it was wrong, and that knowledge would fester like an unhealed scar. The only way to heal my non-existent relationship scar was to give it a lot of time and distance to close. Maybe last time I didn't give it enough time.

I didn't know how to end it without just ending it, so I called him.

"Hi," I said softly. I gave myself a boost of self-confidence by saying it would be better this way.

"Hi," he said. I sensed he already knew it was coming. I could tell by the sound of his voice. My self-doubt lingered. He always let me do it. He never put an end to us.

I wanted to tell him about everything that happened after he left the last time I saw him at my house. I realized I didn't feel comfortable sharing my lost fetus with anyone. I wanted to share what happened with the twins, but I knew I'd have to make it short or I would open up again, and I didn't want to.

"I know I've done this before, but I am ending it with us for good this time," I said.

"Okaaaaay," he said, long and drawn out. "Are you okay?"

"Yeah, I'm fine." I wasn't fine. I was anything but fine.

I told him about everything that happened in court, and what I decided to do. How things had been going and what was about to happen. He was happy that it all turned out.

"So, you don't want to see me anymore?" he said.

"No, I don't because I'm weak when you're with me. I need space, Adam, I need to give myself time to find out who I am. We can still keep in contact through email, but please don't ask to see me. Let's just move on with our lives."

"Okay, maybe it's best. Good luck with everything you'll be going through, Susan. You're an amazing woman."

I wasn't surprised that he gave in so easily. He made it clear early on he didn't want to leave his wife, his job, his kids, his life. He chose his life and wanted what he wanted.

"Thank you." I took a breath and said, "Bye." I was relieved. It was time to move on.

28

Making A Family

With a hint of spring in the air a few weeks into February, I got into my car to drive to Lauren and Tracey's office to meet with the first couple interested in adopting the twins.

I made a quick stop by Lauren's to drop off the twins with her housekeeper, Maria. I knocked on the door and waited for her to hear me, but I doubted she could. No one could ever hear a knock at this extra-large, heavy metal front door with no windows. It had to be four inches thick and looked like a medieval dungeon door with a fancy modern swirl pattern on it. Someone wants to remain safe, I thought. I found the doorbell and pushed it, hearing it chime and echo throughout the house.

Maria opened the door with two hands and bowed her head making enough room for me to inch by with the twins. We'd met a few times over the past few months, and I found her to be rather shy and quiet. Her brown eyes looked sweet and soft. She couldn't have been more than five feet tall. Lauren told me that her daughter Jennifer adored Maria and that she'd been working with her family for years.

"Hola," she said.

"Hola, hello," I said and followed her down the humongous

spiral stairway into the house and to the kitchen area. The ceilings were high and exquisite. Colorful modern art adorned the tall walls.

"Here," she said, and pointed to where all the baby stuff was off the kitchen and into the living area.

"Okay, thank you." The twins were fast asleep in their car seats. I set them down and looked off into the kitchen noticing two extra-large refrigerators and four ovens with granite-lined counters that went around the whole kitchen. I had no idea how many could be seated at their dining room table, maybe forty to fifty people.

"Sí, here is okay." She nodded to let me know it was okay to leave the twins where I put them. I looked around and saw all of the things Lauren had bought for Megan. It looked like a small lacy, pink, girly nursery.

I'd get lost in this house—okay semi-mansion, I thought. I didn't even know what defined a mansion. I wished the boys and I owned our own home, even a little one.

Maria didn't speak much English, but Lauren reassured me that she had many children of her own and was wonderful with babies. She seemed to have a lot of grandmotherly experience. She'd been watching the twins while we went on our court visits, but I had no idea what Lauren told her about what we were all going through.

She pointed at Matthew and said, "Clothes for boy?"

I pulled the diaper bag off my shoulder from the hospital with extra clothes for the twins and laid it next to Lauren's black leather Prada diaper bag.

"Yes, here they are. Thank you so much for all you've done for the twins." I said. She looked at me graciously, and bowed her head.

I found my way out of Lauren's home and headed to the agency.

On my way to Tracey and Lauren's office, I felt a huge sense of relief that we were finally done with the court system. We made our last visit to the courthouse meaningful when Michael and Jackie signed over their parental rights. It made me the first surrogate to become the natural legal mother to children, who I gave birth to but who were not biologically related to me. The courts called it *Adoption through Surrogacy* so the Department of Children and Family Services could process the paperwork.

The final court document read: *"Susan Ring, be adjudged to be the natural and legal mother of the children born in November 2001 and is granted sole and exclusive care and custody of said children."*

Legally, it was officially over!

There would be one hearing to officiate the adoption once I chose parents, and they would include the official adoption at that time as well. The courts approved an order requested by the attorneys to fulfill the remainder of my surrogacy contract fee from where Michael and Jackie stopped making payments and thus had breached our contract. The remainder was supposed to be paid by the new parents. They weren't sure how it would turn out because it had never been requested through the courts before. I didn't get my hopes up. It really made me mad that Michael and Jackie were going to get out of everything. The only wonderful thing, the most important thing would be that the twins would have a home.

Now it was time to find the twins a home, but I could barely breathe.

I didn't understand my emotions. This was why I fought for them. Why did it suddenly feel so wrong?

When I walked into Tracey and Lauren's office, everyone was already there in the middle of the large room facing each other, sitting in office chairs with no table in between. Tracey and Lauren were talking with the couple and didn't stop when I came in the room. It felt strange, like I was late but I wasn't. My chair was in the middle, with Tracey and Lauren on each side of me, with the couple facing us. Tracey pointed to the open chair for me to sit down on. I sat. The setup felt awkward.

I couldn't remember if I was even introduced to the couple sitting across from me. I knew why they were there, but that was all I knew about them.

I simply can't remember a lot from this meeting. I was in the weirdest mood.

The intended adoptive parents prepared a six-page story of their lives that included why they wanted children, and that they had tried for years to have a child but only had disappointment. It felt to me like they were done looking and had high expectations for this meeting. They were close friends of Dr. Kazman, my OB-GYN who was also good friends of Lauren's.

Alice was an attorney, medium height with short blonde hair, articulate, and neatly dressed in a plain off-white dress with matching pointy shoes. Phil was a famous television producer. He looked like one, the type I've seen in Hollywood with thick black glasses, dressed impeccably in his suit. He seemed like a warm individual. I didn't know him by name, but did know the successful television program he created, wrote, and directed.

I was a little turned off with them after five minutes. I wanted to like them, but it seemed like they only talked about surface things, not who they really were, and they weren't talking with me at all. I had prepared a handful of what I thought were deep questions including asking them what unconditional love meant to them. I kept trying to focus so I could give them the benefit of the doubt, but something was off and it just seemed to get worse. I didn't want to ask them the questions I'd prepared. I was trying to figure out why I was so pissed off. I felt like an outcast, a stranger in this conversation. It seemed the decision for them to be the chosen parents was made before I entered the room.

"Oh, yes, we would plan to hire a nanny for the twins," Alice said answering a question from Tracey.

Did that mean they would have a nanny take care of the twins most of the time? How involved would they be as parents?

"We've been waiting so long and feel very good about this adoption after talking to Tracey and Lauren." Phil looked at me briefly and smiled at Lauren and Tracey. "We are so happy you let them take care of the twins for you. You were lucky to have them," he said to me with a smile.

"Wait a minute, what?" I said, sure they saw the surprised look on my face. My heart dropped. Again! "What do you mean? The part about Lauren and Tracey?"

"They took care of the twins for you," Phil said looking over at Alice.

"No, no they didn't. I don't understand." I tried to manage my words, but they came out short and abrupt.

"Yes, so let's move on to the next question, shall we?" Lauren said.

I couldn't believe they would say such a thing. I didn't want to continue the conversation and I never got a copy of the checklist of questions they made up. But I realized my anger was geared toward Lauren and Tracey, not Alice and Phil. Were they supposed to be better caretakers than I was? I had no words except the ones I was familiar with; Shamed, let down, and shocked. They wanted me to feel like the helpless surrogate rescued by rich agency owners or they wanted to show a perfect picture of their own concocted story. Now I knew why they wanted me to sign them over when I first brought them home. Lauren looked at me briefly and then at Tracey. Great, now everyone was uncomfortable. Alice and Phil looked at each other, confused.

I was done. I was hurt and sick of Lauren and Tracey's made-up world. I wondered what they had said when I wasn't there.

I got up from my chair and said, "I'm sorry. I need to go." I briefly looked at the couple before glancing at Lauren and Tracey, and then I walked out.

"I need to go, to get out of here," I stammered. I didn't care what any of them thought. Tracey came down the hall after me.

"Susan! Susan!"

I kept walking. I had enough of their shit and their fancy world. I headed for the glass doors to the lobby.

"Susan, you can't keep them!" Tracey stopped walking in the hall as I pushed the doors open.

"Fuck it," I said softly to myself. Did she even get it at all?

I headed over to pick up the twins. Keeping them with us crossed my mind several times, but I knew it wasn't best for me, or the twins. They were never my babies to begin with. After I picked them up, I drove up and down Main Street near the ocean to reflect on all I'd been through. The ocean had a way of calming me, all I had to do was see it, be near it, and I felt good again. I knew it was time to let go, time to say goodbye.

Lauren called me later that day and I wanted to know why she said what she did, "Why didn't you include me in on your talk with the potential couple?"

"We thought we had the perfect couple Susan. They personally know your doctor and are very well off in the community."

"That doesn't matter to me. What matters is that you lied. Again. Then you both decided without me. Again." I said.

"We're sorry. We have more profiles to look at. So you don't want this couple?"

"I didn't say that. I believe it would be good to look at several and then decide. Not just do this in one day, with one couple." I said.

I decided to ignore the fact that Lauren and Tracey thought they knew better because I knew we'd be done soon.

I had to keep putting one foot in front of the other, and get this done. Then let go.

After giving me a few more profiles of potential adoptive parents to look through, Lauren and Tracey set up another meeting. I tried to clear my head to get in a good place. I wasn't sure I'd find the perfect parents, but I hoped I'd know when it was right.

One of the last couples we met with was Kathy and Russell, who had been married for twelve years. Russell worked for Disney, and Kathy worked with her mother, sister, and father in a home jewelry business. They lived about forty-five minutes away. I was touched when Kathy brought her mother and her sister with her for the interview.

Kathy and Russell had been through twelve unsuccessful IVF procedures, two of which were with a surrogate. They'd just given up trying to have their own children a few weeks before. When they decided to try to adopt, their attorney told them they would probably have to wait at least a year until a baby came up for adoption.

The minute they walked in the agency, Lauren, Tracey, and I could not stop staring at them. "Hello, please come in." Lauren said. They must have felt awkward, because we were whispering to each other, but what we were saying was, "Oh, my God! Kathy looks just like Megan, dark hair, light skin and the same over all features, and Matthew is fair with lighter brownish hair like Russell!" The three of us couldn't stop talking about it.

"I wanted my whole family here, but my dad couldn't make it. He's working. I hope you don't mind," Kathy said. I studied her mother, sister and husband. I could tell she was incredibly nervous.

"I heard about this strange story through my infertility group about a surrogate mother who had given birth to healthy boy and girl twins and that they were looking for a good home," Kathy said, drying her dark brown eyes. "I didn't believe it, thinking it was just another disappointment. I can't believe it's true." Her mother put her arm around Kathy.

We talked for a while and after we all got more comfortable with each other, I asked some of my prepared questions.

"What do you think about unconditional love?" I asked. I was ready to ask several more questions as well.

"It's everything," Kathy said. "You love with no conditions."

There were no exact answers to my questions. I just wanted

them to know that I gave a lot of thought to my few questions and that it mattered to me. We talked for hours and I knew they were the ones. It felt right. Tracey and Lauren wanted me to tell them right after the meeting, but I told them I wanted to make the decision myself, when I was ready. Lauren and Tracey seemed like they were trying very hard to move the process along quickly.

I learned later that Kathy brought her mother and sister because she wanted them to remember what was said in the meeting. She wanted to remember everything so she could answer everything right and improve their chances of adopting the twins.

Through our daily routine as a family, I spent the next few days saying goodbye to the twins.

It was almost as if I did another surrogacy in making a new family.

On a sunny Sunday morning, I called Kathy and Russell. All I could do was trust that they would be the best parents for the twins.

Trust and let go again.

"Hi, Kathy? This is Susan. I met you a few days ago." It felt awkward to say those words. I wanted to think I knew them as people, to know who they would be in ten or twelve years and then choose, but it didn't work that way.

"Hi, Susan, hold on, let me get Russell on the phone too," Kathy said. "We're just having breakfast, hold on." I heard a parrot in the background.

Both of them came on the line. "Okay we're here," Kathy said.

"How are you?" Russell asked.

"I'm good, thanks." I let out a big sigh. "I've called you to let you know that the twins would love to talk to their new mommy and daddy." The twins were in a talkative mood babbling and cooing loudly as I held up the phone for them to hear. My eyes watered as I held back my emotion, waiting to hear what they said.

"What? Oh my God! What?" Kathy exclaimed and I heard her start to cry.

"This is all we've ever wanted," Russell said. The emotion felt overwhelming. They were happy and couldn't wait to meet their children. We still had legal hoops to jump through but they should be cleared through the attorneys soon. It occurred to me that they hadn't even seen pictures of the twins because I decided I didn't want to show any pictures until we were done with the meetings. I think all of us realized things were moving very quickly.

After the phone call, I sent pictures to Kathy and Russell, who were in love with their new daughter and son. They called me back to tell me how excited they were to get their family started. After all of the formalities, and background checks were completed, we set up a meeting time at my house so Kathy and Russell could pick up the twins. It only took a few weeks. The twins were just shy of three months old.

A new family of four was born. And I felt a gaping hole in my life.

Russell and Kathy came over to our house on a Saturday morning in February 2002. Brian and Steven were at baseball practice, and Terrie and I were home. I explained to the boys that the twins had new parents and they'd be going home with them while they were at practice. I said it wasn't goodbye because they'd see the twins again, but they wouldn't be here when they came home.

I set up fresh flowers on the center of the dining room table with pictures of Brian and Steven to warm the room. I added the photo albums my mother had personally designed and made for Megan and Matthew on the same table, and filled them with pictures of the babies for their new mommy and daddy. I gathered up their belongings and clothes, Mickey and Minnie Mouse, toys, ID bracelets, binkies, pictures of their footprints at birth, birth certificates, and Social Security numbers. They were dressed in little soft pink and blue teddy bear outfits. Seventeen years later, I can still see those outfits in my mind's eye.

Kathy sat on the couch, opened her arms and said, "Oh my God, Susan, they are beautiful," awestruck as I handed her, first Megan and then Matthew into her other arm. Russell looked on with tears coming down his cheeks.

I smiled and looked at Terrie. I took in the moment. It was bittersweet. It was Russell's turn to hold them both at the same time. He smiled and said, "Wow," as I filled his arms with their new son and daughter. The looks on Russell's and Kathy's faces are something I will never forget.

"We were thinking of new names the other day," Kathy said.

I felt my stomach flip, and my heart felt heavy but knew if I was adopting, I would probably want to choose the names of my children, too. That didn't make it hurt any less.

We visited for a few hours, and it was time for them to go. After they left Terrie said, "It's okay to cry, Susan,"

I half smiled. "No, I'm happy for them, Ter." We hugged and I said, "Thank you, thank you for being who you are and being here when I needed you most." "You're welcome." She went to her room and I wandered back to the front door to see if I could see the new family.

I watched from my door as they finished putting the twins into their car seats and packed all the stuff in the car. Boomer sat at my feet and looked up at me. I patted him on the head and he slid down on his front legs and let out a big sigh. "It's okay, boy." I leaned down to pat him on the head again.

"There goes a piece of my heart," I said to Boomer. I couldn't look away and stared out the door watching them drive off to their new life.

We went about our day. I knew it was okay to cry, but all I felt was numb. The days following were quiet, and felt exactly like they did after Evan's delivery. I missed the twins terribly and waited for the tears but they didn't come. I wished they would. I tried to make myself cry but couldn't. Numbness and sadness filled my heart. I knew to move forward, and go on with my own life.

The court hearing to finalize the adoption was thirty days after Kathy and Russell picked up the twins, officially marking the twins' legal adoption. The judge ruling the original case was to also hold the adoption hearing.

In the meantime, I met with DCFS to go through all the adoption steps and filled out the paperwork on background for me, and the twins. Michael filled out his part as well, and the caseworker gave me a copy of what he filled out. A woman from DCFS came out to my house a few days later to do an inspection of my home and visit with me. She looked exactly like the lady who showed up in court. It might have been her, but I didn't ask.

"You can go down to the home office in downtown Los Angeles and sign the final paperwork if you'd like to get things moving along faster," she said as we were sitting at the dining room table with a stack of paper in front of her.

"No, this way is fine. I'm okay with the timing. I won't change my mind." I got up from the table.

"Okay, but it puts the new parents at ease if you consider it." She stood.

"I'm good, thank you." I didn't want to go all the way downtown just to sign paperwork. She left with all the signed off paperwork.

It felt more natural to just let time slip by to make it official.

29

A Final Request

The early morning sun peeked through the living room drapes as I sat on the couch unable to sleep, drinking coffee by myself. It was the end of the first week without the twins and it was quiet in our home. The boys were still sleeping and I didn't know what to do with myself.

I wondered if I made the right choice and guessed I may never know. How does anyone choose parents within an hour or two of meeting someone? It was a life-altering decision for the twins and me. I already learned from personal experience that you could know someone for years and never really know who they are until things go wrong. All I could do was choose the best I knew how, trust, and let it go, but it was harder than I thought.

I hoped Kathy and Russell would stay in touch. I tried to keep a distance from the twins so I could leave them when I did. I gave myself more than enough time to say goodbye. I spent time with just the two of them, reminding myself to slow down and try not to get too close, but I felt like I failed miserably.

Something was missing.

I thought about them all the time. I went to my bedroom

and thought it would be a good idea to move my furniture around. I moved my bed to the other side of the room and found a pacifier under my bed. I held it to my cheek and then put it in my drawer for my keepsake box. I wished Kathy and Russell would call to let me know how the twins were. They felt as close to me as the blood rushing through my veins. I missed them so much.

I stayed in these feelings alone because I didn't know how to share them. On the outside, I felt like my life had reverted back to normal. I was a mother to two kids with a daycare. But sometimes I could still hear the twins crying and saw myself get up and change their diapers, change their clothes, and cuddle them close.

My eye doctor's office called to let me know an appointment opened up for a pterygium surgery I needed that I'd put off several times because I couldn't find the time. I took the first appointment and scheduled the eye surgery for the next day.

The doctor's office was adamant about having a driver after the surgery, but I didn't have one, so I lied and said I had someone waiting outside. I made my way out of the back door to get to my car, feeling like a thief and liar on the run. I was mad at myself for lying, but Terrie was busy at work and I was too proud to ask anyone else. I caught a quick glance of my eyes in the rear view mirror and scared myself, feeling the pulsing pressure within my eyeballs. I popped a few Advil and drove very carefully home after resting for an hour in the car. It was a short drive.

An hour after I got home, I made my way to the bathroom and looked at my eyes. They looked horrible. The doctor scraped the pupils of the yellowy gristle out of both eyes and they were now blood red with no white showing. I was told they would get better in a few days, but I looked like a zombie vampire. I felt like all hints of my identity were gone.

Later that day I walked over to pick up the kids from school with my sunglasses on.

I explained to the kids earlier about how my eyes were going to look post op and told them again after school.

"Okay, my eyes are going to look really awful, but don't worry they will go back to normal in a few days," I told the kids as we walked home.

They looked at me like I was kidding.

"Guys, I'm serious," I said, because I didn't want to scare the crap out of them. "I don't want to scare you, so I'm going to show you now, and then keep my sunglasses on. Okay?" The boys and day care kids shook their heads, waiting for the gore.

"Okay, Mom...Susan," they all said.

I pulled off my glasses so they could see my eyes. I saw their whole bodies cringe. "Ohhhhhh, my God!" they cried, along with "Ew!" and "That's scary!" They laughed at the gory part. "What a great Halloween costume," one of the boys said.

It was gross and got worse before it got better, so I kept my sunglasses on inside and outside. Making things worse, puss oozed out of the corner of my eyes.

Kathy called the next day to tell me how the twins were doing. I was at home resting, hoping my eyes would look better by the end of the day. They looked a little better than the day before.

"How are you guys?" I asked, happy to know she called just to let me know how things were going. I wanted to know all about how their new family was acclimating. I heard one of the twins babbling in the background and I smiled.

"Oh, they are doing great, Susan. They are a lot of work," she said, but I could tell she wasn't complaining.

"Yes, that is true, Kathy. A lot."

Although she sounded happy, I could tell she had something she wanted to ask me.

"So, Susan...I have a favor to ask you."

"Sure, what is it?"

"Our attorney said there are papers you can sign to relinquish your rights sooner as the twins' legal mother. It would mean the world to us if you could go down to DCFS and sign your rights away… today."

I felt cornered but knew all of it would be done at the hearing in less than thirty days anyway.

"I can do it next week, Kathy. I just had surgery on my eyes yesterday."

"Surgery? Are you okay?"

"Yeah, I'm fine. Pterygiums, yellow gunk in my eyes from the sun." I sighed.

"Please, Susan, we really want to get the paperwork moving now. It will move things along faster. The papers are ready for you at DCFS in Los Angeles," she said, excited.

I knew it was because she was worried about me changing my mind. I wasn't going to change my mind, but I knew it would make Kathy and Russell feel better if I signed away my rights early.

"Okay. I'll see what I can do."

I've done a lot of stupid things in my life, but driving to downtown Los Angeles the day after eye surgery on a Friday was not yet one of them. Everything told me not to get into the car, but I wanted Kathy to know I wouldn't let her and Russell down. Maybe this would give me hope to move along faster in my life. I knew that all my choices would be gone once I signed the papers, so I decided to go.

As stupid as it was, I did it. Friday traffic mid-morning was as good as L.A. traffic gets so I targeted that time. I figured no one would see my eyes if I kept my sunglasses on. All I had to do was sign and leave. "Sign and leave," I repeated aloud.

30

The Unexpected Mother

I made my way to the DCFS office in Los Angeles. The overcast sky made it hard to see the address on the tall building. I opened the door to the office and was welcomed by a receptionist with blonde hair swept back into a petite bun. She was gathering her things to leave probably for an early lunch, I thought.

"Hi, I'm here to sign adoption papers. My name is…"

"Oh yes, hello. No need to introduce yourself. It's such a pleasure to meet you, Susan," she said. "I've read all the paperwork about your case and thought it was wonderful of you to come to the office to sign away your parental rights for the new parents."

I smiled and felt a light burn in my eyes, making them tear up. I wiped the corners and re-adjusted my sunglasses to make sure they were on tight. I had to consciously remember to keep them on.

A man in a light-colored blue and pink crisscross patterned dress shirt and khaki pants greeted me. "Hello, Susan. I will help you through the paperwork process."

He looked at the woman at the desk and said, "Thanks Maggie, I'll take this case." He reached out and we shook hands. He leaned in close and whispered, "My name is Ben and when you make your story into a movie, I'll put in an early request that you make sure Tom Cruise plays me. Okay?"

I laughed softly and smiled. I towered over him and he looked nothing like Tom Cruise. No taller than maybe 5 ft. He had trendy glasses, messy blonde hair, and an excellent sense of humor.

He led me into a conference room with windows all around it that people in offices refer to as "the fish bowl."

"I, um, had eye surgery yesterday, so I need to keep these sunglasses on as we sign, okay?"

"Sure, that's fine," he said. "Two more people—interns—will be joining us so they can learn from the case. Is that okay with you?"

"Sure, that's okay."

"It won't take too long, but I do apologize up front for some of the wording. We don't have paperwork for Adoption via Surrogacy. We only have paperwork for regular, standard biological adoptions.

Two interns came in and sat across the table with Ben. They had notepads and looked eager to learn.

"Sure that's fine. No worries. I'm sure all the wording isn't anything I haven't heard or read already." I prepared myself for his questions trying to remember what DCFS said when they were at my house.

He did a short interview and let the two interns ask questions as well. Most of the questions were ones I had already answered. Ben and the interns left the room. What was supposed to be just signing a piece of paper took close to an hour. I was getting frustrated because my eyes were burning.

I sat by myself at the table thinking about the first time I considered being a surrogate mother. It was the day I gave birth to Brian. After everything that happened with Michael and Jackie, knowing the finality of the surrogacy contract, and now signing away my parental rights made me think about trust. I had no idea that trust would ever come into play. I thought we agreed about everything in the contract and trust would naturally follow. It was supposed to be a two-way street. When I signed my first contract with Michael and Jackie, I thought the second journey would work just like the first one and that we'd never run into these problems. I just assumed this was such an important life-making decision for the intended parents that I automatically trusted them to not change their minds. It never entered my mind that they might not keep their promise to me, let alone the twins.

I knew myself well enough to know I'd be a person they could trust, but they didn't know that, I thought. They didn't know that I would carry their child just like I carried my own. I wondered about the best way to know you can trust a person. There is no way to know for sure, and you certainly can't tell by looking at someone whether you can trust them or not. Sometimes you just have to do it, take the leap, which meant it was okay to hold out your hand and ask for help if you need it. It doesn't make you weak, like I'd always thought.

My mind jolted back to the present when Ben and the interns came back into the conference room.

"Okay, so just a few more questions. This is probably an uncomfortable question for you, so like I said, I do apologize."

I squirmed in my chair wondering what it could possibly be.

"Why are you giving up your children?" Ben asked and put his pen down on the table.

I felt my throat close, and I couldn't breathe. I wanted to cry and felt the tears coming. "Um, because, I um…I wasn't the actual mother, I was a surrogate mother and…" I tried hard to keep a straight face and not cry but it was coming. I was glad my sunglasses were on. He wrote down my answer.

I looked over at the two interns. No one said a word. I swallowed hard.

"There are no right answers, Susan, but I do have to ask the questions."

"Why are you giving up your daughter?" he asked, knowing he hit a nerve. I could tell he felt bad about it, but he was waiting for my answer. My daughter, I thought. I always wanted a daughter. A tear fell from the bottom of my sunglasses onto the table. I didn't say anything and felt a lump in my throat. My throat felt heavy with grief and I couldn't speak. The words were caught inside. I tried to gulp them down again.

"Why are you giving up your son?" he asked before I had a chance to answer the other question. "I'm so sorry, but I have to ask."

I shook my head to let him know it was okay, but I still couldn't answer. I started to say something. I used my hands in front of me to force my words out, but nothing came.

My son, I thought. I would never give up my son. Another tear joined my cheek on the other side and they rolled faster down my face. I sat up straight wishing I were invisible. I felt a tremendous loss, like someone died in front of me. The numbness was gone and my body suddenly felt everything. It felt heavy, loaded with sadness and unbearable guilt. I couldn't breathe or stop the tears.

I thought about the triplet that was reduced. Was it a boy or a girl? I didn't know, and the gender didn't matter to me. The third question might have been, "Why are you giving up your other son or daughter?" or "Why did you let the third one be reduced, murdered, or killed?" I wasn't even sure if they knew about the third one, but I'd never forget. As awful as it all was, I was grateful I had half a choice.

I stood looking for the closest exit. My knees felt weak. I needed to run, get away. My face was wet from tears and I couldn't think. I took off my sunglasses and dabbed my face and eyes with my sleeve. That was when Ben looked at me, horrified. I put my sunglasses back on after I saw his surprised face.

"Are you okay?" he asked staring at my eyes.

"No, I'm not okay," I managed. "Out, I need to get out. Can't breathe. Are we done here?" I breathed in hard not remembering if I breathed out. Don't lose it here, Susan, not here, I thought. Just leave, go outside. Breathe. I wanted to make a break for the elevator.

"Yes, but you need to sign here for Megan and here for Matthew." He pointed to two lines.

I signed both pages with tears dropping onto the scribbled, illegible signature. I took a deep breath and said, "The answers to all of those questions you asked are because I was their surrogate mother, not their mother, and it was all unexpected. I was the unexpected mother."

Ben looked at me with a blank expression. I made my way to the elevator doors. Once there, I hit the down button, waiting impatiently for the elevator to arrive. When it finally came, I hit all the buttons to escape. My eyes watered and were blurry. I couldn't find number 1, the first floor.

I loved the twins and couldn't acknowledge it because it would hurt. I never kept any distance from them and loved them the whole time. Trying to be strong and not giving up made me push the pain away, which was a good place to hide, but I pushed it away so hard that it had to go somewhere. It went deep inside my body like only pain knows how to do. Pain and grief pulled me down, to be with it, to deal with it. It was so heavy I couldn't hold it up. Something crumbled inside. I loved them like they were my own. I sobbed louder at the real thought, the real feeling.

I fell to my knees onto the red concrete brick outside the building and cried harder. My eyes burned and felt gritty, itchy. I couldn't get up. I wanted to go home and cry, away from so many people around me, but I only cried harder. People walked by me, I looked up but I couldn't remember their faces. They walked around me, staring. Still on my knees, I searched for my car.

"Why are you giving up your daughter/son?" kept ringing in my ears.

The reality and truth was that I was their mother and I just gave them up. I was their legal mother in the state of California. I had a son and daughter, and now I didn't. How could I let them go? I knew in my heart I did the right thing, I was just unbelievably sad. When would it feel better?

It felt like every collective thought about giving up a child found its way into my heart. I thought about all the women who came through those doors after giving up their child for adoption for whatever reason.

They were my new heroes.

I had to make it to my car. I lifted myself one foot at a time. "Come on, Susan, you can do it. Get up!" *Breathe*, a voice said inside my head. The front of my shirt was wet from snot and tears. I looked down to pull up my right leg up and blood slowly trickled from my knee through a small hole in my yoga pants.

I walked hunched over and got closer to where I parked my car on Wilshire Boulevard, the busiest street in Los Angeles, hiding my face. I was on the sidewalk near my front bumper searching for my keys. I couldn't find my damn keys, and everything was blurry. My knees buckled and I hit the ground again. Did I leave my keys back in the office where I felt interrogated? I put my purse in my lap and sat on the curb with my arms wrapped around my legs. It was finally okay to cry, so I cried and cried into my knees until I heard a man's voice.

"Are you okay, do you need help?" He parked a silver bicycle in front of me. I looked up and saw his outline in the early afternoon sun. He looked athletic, wearing a yellow biker helmet and skintight clothes that cyclists wear, and dark sun goggles.

"Could you help me up?" I managed to say and took a deep breath wondering why my legs wouldn't hold me up. I surprised myself by asking for help.

"Sure," he said. "Are you okay?" He held me up close while I struggled to stand, then I planted my feet on the ground.

"Yes," I lied. "Well, no." I kept my head down feeling

embarrassed and sobbed through my words. "I gave up my kids, right there at DCFS today." I pointed to the building. "But they weren't really my kids, but they were and…" I'm not even sure he heard what I said because the words came with snot coming out of my nose, and I felt them getting stuck again in my throat.

"You gave up your kids?" he asked slowly, distinctly, unbelievably.

I looked up at him and nodded.

I could see he was concerned. He pulled me to his big manly chest and squeezed hard. He turned his head away from my face and wrapped his strong arms around my upper body. I felt safe and sobbed for what felt like forever. I wanted him to rescue me, but I felt too wounded and embarrassed. I couldn't take off my sunglasses for fear he'd think I was a freak. He held me until my breathing calmed. I smelled his aftershave mixed with sweat, it made me realize how much I missed being with a man. I held onto him, tight.

"You okay now?" He pulled away and took off his goggles. In the bright sunlight I saw the biggest, most beautiful brown eyes with yellow star outlines I'd ever seen.

I nodded. "Yeah, I think so." I kept looking at his eyes and cleared my throat.

"Did you find your keys?"

"No, let me look." I put my head down into my purse.

I opened my bag and saw where I left them.

"Okay, I'll get you into your car, but take your time before you drive. Don't leave until you've calmed down okay?"

"Okay, thank you." I nodded and sniffed in hard. He grabbed the handlebars to his bike and pulled his goggles back on. His brown-skinned fingers held the bars to his bike and I saw his wedding ring, a solid silver band. He put his bike against a pole and helped me into my car.

"Okay? All good?" he asked.

I nodded. "Thank you." He nodded and then smiled and

shut my car door. I sat in silence as I watched him get on his bike and get ready to leave. He looked at me and threw one leg over the seat to the pedal on his bicycle and started to ride away.

This stranger took ten minutes out of his life to help me. It meant more to me than he could ever imagine. There really were people out in the world who I could trust on a whim and lean on to lend a helping hand even in brief encounter, like this guy, real and genuine. It was possible to find this kind of person by being open to it. I realized it was okay to be human and reach out for help when I needed it. I was feeling my own vulnerability. I sat in the car thinking, my mind wandering, and looked out over the city.

In that moment, I realized I did what I set out to do. I made a family.

He turned around a few blocks away at a stop sign and waved. I put my hand up to wave back and followed him with my eyes until I couldn't see him anymore.

Perhaps this all happened for a reason unknown to me, I thought. I breathed in and out, calmly knowing everything was going to be okay. The twins were safe and loved. I took a deep breath in this time, the one I'd been holding since the beginning of my journey, and let it out to move deftly through my body.

I was letting go.

Dear Reader,

I hope you enjoyed *The Unexpected Mother*.

It took me a long time to write this book, twelve years to be exact – five serious ones. As a new writer, it was indeed a labor-of-love to bring out all of my feelings and emotions and put them into book form.

Book two, When Hope Becomes Life is online, and ready to go! It details my next three journeys as a surrogate mother.

And when Oprah called, I was floored.

How did she find out about me?

Oprah wanted my story for her magazine. She asked me a few simple questions.

Why would I want to be a surrogate mother?

Did I sometimes have doubts?

Well, what happened next shocked me, and you'll find out in the second book.

If you enjoyed the first part of my life, you'll love the next bit. I've poured passion into all of my books and I'm just getting started.

Won't you join me in the second book, When Hope Becomes Life?

https://www.amazon.com/When-Hope-Becomes-Life-Surrogate-ebook/dp/B07QHY94Q7

Thank you!

Epilogue

For those of you who don't know, I've been blessed to keep in contact with Megan, Matthew, and their family throughout the years while they've grown up. They are happy, loved, well-adjusted teenagers graduating high school this year and I've been invited! Where does the time go?

I get many requests about the reality of the surrogacy experience because someone seems to always know someone battling infertility. I'm a huge advocate *for* surrogacy. It always has been, and always will be, very near and dear to my heart.

It is my intention in writing this book that it helps bring about surrogacy awareness. I hope it will create more honest communication, and open discussions around the topic of surrogacy. It is life changing for women to express the truth of their power in helping another person have a child.

One last note, if you have feedback about my book and would like to share, please consider leaving a review through your purchase at Amazon or Goodreads. It would be wonderful to hear from you.

Acknowledgements

Evan, Megan, Matthew and Little One, I started this book for you so that you would know the truth about how you came into this world. This book ended up being for me, too, helping me heal in so many ways. Writing it gave me strength and courage to tell my story. I'm only sorry it took so long to write it. Love to you always.

Mom, thank you for giving me life. I miss you so much. I know you loved me in the best way you knew how. The love you gave me as a little girl sustained me enough to make me who I am today. You always believed in me, even when I didn't believe in myself.

My sons, Brian and Steven, I'm so incredibly proud of who you are as humans and young men in today's world. These journeys wouldn't have happened if you didn't openly share your Mom like you did. I love you so very much, and thank you beyond belief for being in my life.

My daughter, Nevaeh, I gave birth to you a little later in life than most moms do, but I know you were brought here for a reason. You're daddy's 'first' child, my 'first' daughter, and for both of us our second family. You've added more love into my life than I ever imagined possible. Love you.

My lover, friend, and husband Paul, to say thank you seems so small and not enough. You stood by me as I let my secrets out one by one, and you loved me anyway. I grew more as a person and learned how to be a partner in our marriage. I'm grateful to you beyond measure, because without you in my life and supporting me the way you have this book might never have been written. I know intimate love with you.

Terrie, my friend for being there with me through thick and thin for so long! I'm so eternally grateful for our long and loving friendship. You mean the world to me. Love you always.

My brothers, my sisters, you guys are awesome, and I love you all so much. Grateful beyond belief that you agreed to read my manuscript right after I wrote it. You gave me everything I needed to move on, and tell my truth.

My extended family and friends, thank you for being in my life. I love you.

Hugh Howey and 20Booksto50, thank you for paving the way for independent (Indie) writers of all genres. I spent many hours on your websites learning the how-to. You were a huge inspiration to me, as a writer, in so many ways. It was a pleasure meeting you Hugh, in Redondo Beach on your 2013 book tour, and 20Booksto50 I'm always with you in paying it forward.

E-harmony, thank you for being the matching device that helped me find Paul, my husband, when I was forty-nine years old. We were both fed up with the dating online services, and it was both of our last dates when we found each other through your site.

My Readers, thank you for taking time out of your life to come into my world for a brief time. As a voracious reader myself, it's readers like you who make it happen. Thank you!

About The Author

Susan Ring lives in Orange County, California with her daughter, Nevaeh and husband Paul, with two very interactive cats. Susan's two grown boys, Brian and Steven, reside in Los Angeles, CA.

If you would like to visit Susan, you can check out her new website at www.susanaring.com